CONTENTS

REVOLUTIONARY ★ GENEROSITY

KIRK NOWERY

FOREWORD BY JOHN C. MAXWELL

Copyright © 2006 by Spire Publishing

Published by Spire Resources Inc.
PO Box 180
Camarillo, CA 93011
1-800-992-3060

Unless otherwise noted Scripture quotations are taken from the
HOLY BIBLE: NEW INTERNATIONAL VERSION®. Copyright ©
1973, 1978, 1984 by International Bible Society. Used by permission of Zondervan Publishing House.

Cover and text design by Bill Thielker

Printed in the United States of America

ACKNOWLEDGMENTS

A dozen years ago, Dr. John C. Maxwell asked me, "Do you have a heart for pastors?" I immediately answered *Yes*, and then I added that, to me, having a heart *for* pastors begins with understanding the heart *of* a pastor. A pastoral heart is a heart of service, a heart that is yielded to God and open to people. Dr. Maxwell told me that his heart for pastors motivated him to be a value-adder to their lives and ministries. After working with him for over a decade I can affirm enthusiastically that John C. Maxwell truly does add value to people's lives. He has blessed me in that way, and I will always be grateful for the opportunities and friendship he has given me.

I also want to express to Andy Stimer, my co-writer and editor, my deepest thanks for his intellectual investment in our ministry and his personal investment in my life. His ability to think and dream with me as a friend and mentor has left a lasting imprint on my mind and heart.

In Dr. Maxwell's book, *The 21 Irrefutable Laws of Leadership*, one of the principles is called *The Law of the Inner Circle*. It says: You can rise no higher than the people around you. How true this is! To my senior leadership team at ISS I want to express my thanks for your commitment to me and to the development of this ministry that God has given us. You have breathed life into me as we strive to honor God in all we do, to develop people, and to do everything with excellence.

Last, and most importantly, I want to thank my family. Denise and I have had the honor (with God's immeasurable help) to raise three children, all now adults, who are true leaders and who exemplify what it means to "take hold of the life that is truly life." They represent the core of this book's teachings. I thank God for them.

FOREWORD

As I write these words I am on the verge of turning 60. For the past three decades I have been committed to *making a difference with people who make a difference doing something that makes a difference at a time that makes a difference*. Today, as I approach another of life's major mileposts, I am modifying that statement slightly. For the next decade, I am determined with God's enablement to make a difference with *leaders* who make a difference. Instead of practicing addition, I want to practice multiplication; for only in multiplying can I make the most significant contribution through my life. In light of this insightful new book by my friend and colleague Kirk Nowery, I would have to say that I want to make a *revolutionary* contribution. I hope that is your desire, too. If it is, this book will inspire you greatly and instruct you richly.

Revolutionaries are often misunderstood and their impact sometimes skips a generation. In my book, *The Difference Maker*, I relate a story about one of history's true revolutionaries, Christopher Columbus. On August 3, 1492, Columbus set sail from the port of Palos in southern Spain in search of a western route to Asia. He was convinced that the world was round, despite the widespread belief that the world was flat. The majority of people in Europe believed that a ship sailing due west would ultimately fall off the edge of the earth!

On that historic voyage Columbus did not find the route he sought, but he did confirm his suspicions that the earth is a sphere. After months of exploration and the loss of only one ship, he returned to Spain on March 15, 1493. The nation welcomed him as a hero, a man of daring who had conquered the seas. He was praised for having survived his grand venture. He was hailed as a discoverer of new lands. But no matter how much he said to the contrary, people continued to believe that the earth is flat. Columbus spent the rest of his life declaring that the earth is round while nearly everyone of his generation went on believing the opposite. It wasn't until the succeeding generations that such a "radical" idea was accepted as fact.

This book brilliantly sets forth a case for revolutionary living. Kirk writes of the priority of wholehearted commitment, the price of sacrificial service, and the high calling of bold witness for Jesus Christ. He lays out principles and presents some amazing stories. I'm sure there will be people like those in Columbus' day who think, "It just can't be that way" and decide to go on following the same pattern, thinking the same thoughts. I hope that you will be different, that you will take to heart these extraordinary things and put the principles into practice. I know that I will, and I'm grateful for this clarion call to a life that makes a revolutionary difference.

John C. Maxwell
Atlanta, GA

INTRODUCTION

It was July 2005. I don't recall the exact date, but I'll never forget the moment. One night, just after midnight, the Spirit of God began to lead our family to a place of faith we had never been to before. He was calling me and calling my wife Denise to willingly surrender to Him our most precious gifts, our children.

The mere thought—*Would you be willing?*—generated profound emotions in me. It was something I had never felt before that moment. I'm not sure how I would have handled it alone; but Denise and I were in it together.

I had just celebrated 10 years working alongside Dr. John C. Maxwell in the company he founded to help pastors and churches, INJOY Stewardship Services. By that 10th year together we had partnered with over 3,000 congregations in every state and several foreign countries. I was feeling tired and worn, a feeling shared by our entire team of ministry specialists and consultants. Constant travel to churches from coast to coast had proven to be very different from the life I had lived as a pastor in South Florida. It had been 20 years in the pastorate followed by 10 years as a "pastor to pastors." By comparison, the first 20 years were much easier than the next 10.

I was turning 50 at the time, and it seemed that

several streams were emptying into the decision pool of my life. I had just read John Maxwell's book, *The Success Journey,* a book he had written when he turned 50. Dr. Maxwell made one statement in particular that helped me to focus my priorities. He wrote, "I made a decision to go from investing in people generally to investing in leaders specifically." About that same time I heard him tell a group of business executives, "People don't remember what you do at the beginning of your life, they remember what you do at the end of your life...so finish well." After 10 years of working with him, I can tell you that John is the real deal! He is genuinely spiritual, absolutely consistent, and unwaveringly faithful. I listen very carefully when he says something like that, and I take it to heart.

In the convergence of influences that came together in the summer of 2005 another major factor was my decade-long friendship with Franklin Graham, president of the relief organization Samaritan's Purse and leader of his father's organization, The Billy Graham Evangelistic Association. Franklin and I were kindred spirits with similar passions—a love for Alaska, for our children and for the spread of the Gospel. The previous year I had traveled with Franklin into the rugged wilderness of the Alaskan Range, flying a bush plane to a remote camp. My son Matthew had joined us on that trip; and he and Franklin proved to be kindred spirits, too.

Back to that night in July 2005...

It was half past midnight when the phone rang. It was Franklin calling, and he was obviously wide awake (in total contrast to my grogginess, having been jarred out of a sound sleep). We talked for just a few minutes, but it was a turning point. In the first chapter of this book I give the details of our conversation and what ensued from our brief exchange. It was the beginning of an extraordinary journey that continues to this day, a journey that has changed me, changed my wife, and radically altered the lives of our three children, Ashley, Clint and Matt.

Denise and I have taken our kids on great adventures from the time they were toddlers all the way into young adulthood. We've been all over the world—to Asia, Europe, Africa, and throughout the Americas. We've climbed mountains, hunted big game and fished the great oceans. But more importantly, we have rolled up our sleeves and gotten involved in ministries to people of all ages, races and stations in life. We've taken the love of Jesus everywhere from the slums of Nairobi to the Amazon basin of South America. Today, all three of our children are wholeheartedly committed to Christ. They are living lives of revolutionary dedication, and for that reason I tell some of their stories in this book. My own legacy will be best expressed in what they do and in who they are. They are the sum of years of daily decisions, long talks, unbounded love and a determination to embody the character of Christ.

In the past year especially I have been asked often, *How did you raise these kids?* Of course, the first and most obvious answer is that they have a phenomenal mother. She is amazing. And Denise and I have always had the same perspective on our children— that they are gifts from God, never an inconvenience, never a burden. Every passion we felt in serving the Lord we wanted them to feel, too. Our determination was to stay on fire for God and to keep them as close to that fire as possible. Along the journey, God has been so good in bringing into our lives so many wonderful people who interacted with our kids and gave them positive influences beyond the scope of our family. I think of my mom and dad who loved them so, and people like the Murphys, the Wootens, players from the Miami Dolphins, the Lewises, the Prevos, the Stimers, the Janneys, myriad teachers and coaches, and great friends from our church in Miami and our company in Atlanta. And, of course, John and Margaret Maxwell, who have always welcomed them, always encouraged them.

When my friend Andy Stimer and I began talking about this book project we had both been thinking in a similar vein. In fact, it was uncanny how similar our thoughts were; and as we began the process of researching and preparing to write it became clear that the theme of revolution was predominant. We couldn't get away from the revolutionary nature of Christ's example, expressed through seven key elements of a spiritually revolutionary life. Each one is connected to the others in ways both obvious and subtle. I can assure you, if you embrace these seven ideals, if you determine to live them to the full, you will experience your own personal revolution. And you will have a lasting impact on the people in your sphere of influence.

The New Testament describes the imperative of going "from faith to faith"[1]—constantly growing in Christ, ever moving to the next level. That is the essence of revolutionary commitment, and that is where this book begins.

Throughout this book are stories of men, women, youth and even children who are living radically effective lives. One in particular I have left to mention in this introduction because his example was so extraordinary. Ron Lewis—pastor, teacher, thinker, strategist, futurist, counselor—was an unforgettable character. He was a man of great vision and formidable faith. On his last night of this earthly life I walked into his hospital room, finding him in tremendous pain, tubes running in and out of his body. Ravaged with cancer, he still managed to smile and greet me warmly. My thoughts took me back in that instant to the day Ron told me he was dying. Actually, what he told me was that he knew he was in for a struggle, but "right around the next corner there's a new dream to dream."

In that sterile hospital room we were far removed from the thousands of people whose lives he had touched, the throngs to whom he had preached, the hundreds of pastors he had guided so sagely. There was only his family—the love of his life, Sue, his son Scott of whom he was so proud, his beloved daughter Kelly and her husband Mark, and his grandchildren. Ron called me to his side and gripped my arm with surprising strength. He asked me to lean over so that I could hear his feeble words. With a voice that was almost a whisper, he prayed for me, asking God to help me keep dreaming big dreams, to keep pressing forward in faith. Ron was about to experience the reality that "to be absent from the body is to be present with the Lord." He was about to graduate to heaven. But before he did, he asked everyone in the room to be near him, and he prayed for each one. He was still giving encouragement, still lifting up every person in the circle of his life. And then he was gone.

Ron Lewis was a revolutionary. When I ponder the meaning of revolutionary commitment, witness, servanthood and generosity, his picture fits perfectly into those frames. On the day he died Ron said, "My passion is to enlarge the boundaries of heaven and enrich the lives of believers." He left a legacy that inspires me to see every day as a gift and to seize every opportunity to serve Jesus Christ and guide others to know him and follow him.

My prayer and hope is that this book will challenge you to a truly revolutionary life—a barrier-breaking life that will matter for all eternity.

Your fellow revolutionary,

R. Kirk Nowery
Atlanta, GA

1

Revolutionary Commitment

Putting Your Life on the Line

"**I** have seen the most horrible things, but I have met people who are still full of faith in spite of what they've endured."

That was the opening statement to a joint gathering of leaders and supporters of Samaritan's Purse and the Billy Graham Evangelistic Association. The speaker was my son, Matthew Nowery, who serves with Samaritan's Purse in Sudan, the most dangerous place in all of Africa and perhaps the entire world. His speech continued, "Eighteen months ago I was at home, a recent graduate of the University of Georgia waiting on an opportunity, looking for a place to commit my life." Matt then turned to face Franklin Graham, president of Samaritan's Purse and son of renowned evangelist Billy Graham. "Mr. Graham," he said, "this is the first time since the day you gave me the opportunity in Sudan that I have been able to thank you publicly. So, tonight, in front of all these people, I want to say thank you for challenging a young man like me." Matt then expressed gratitude to his director in Africa, Scott Hughett, and to his teammates—four other young men who put their lives on the line every day in the cause of Christ.

Matt went on to tell the stories of three Sudanese pastors who had been tortured in front of their wives and children. Each man had been beaten repeatedly and cautioned to not continue their church work. Yet each one refused to obey the oppressors, and each one paid the high price of devotion to Christ. Matthew described the remarkable things he had seen in just a year and a half—

Each one refused to obey the oppressors, and each one paid the high price of devotion.

unspeakable scenes of human misery in a place where millions have been killed and millions more swept into a sea of refugees. Getting very specific, Matt said, "My team and I have recorded the stories of 429 Christian pastors who have been tortured and martyred in Sudan. In most cases, their church buildings were destroyed, sometimes burned down with the church members locked inside. The Christians are victims in a reign of violence driven by the fierce Muslim government of the north. They have been persecuted severely, and many have died, but others are waiting to take their place." At the end of his speech, Matt walked over to the edge of the stage where Franklin Graham was seated. "Mr. Graham," he said, "Thank you again for challenging me, for asking me to make a difference, for calling on me to make my life count for the kingdom. Please don't ever stop challenging young people!"

As my wife Denise and I listened to Matt speak that night, our hearts were filled with pride and our eyes with tears. The boy we had raised had become a man, fully committed to Jesus Christ, wholeheartedly dedicated to communicating His love, truth, grace and saving power. Matt had come to understand the primacy and urgency of the Gospel. It caused us to think back over the years of raising him and our other children, Ashley and Clint. In one of those odd life-flashing-before-your-eyes moments I recalled the day our journey into parenthood began.

Denise and I hadn't been married very long when she announced to me one day that she was pregnant. Together we announced the news to my parents, and my dad had his own announcement: "It is *definitely* a boy" he said, "because the Nowerys don't have girls." And then he went further out on a limb: "In fact, we don't have boys...we have *men*." Some months later we were gathered in the waiting area at the hospital, eagerly anticipating a report from the delivery room. I was waiting along with everyone else because that was back when it was still uncommon for the husband to be present for the childbirth. At last, the doctor stepped into the room with a big smile on his face and said, "Kirk, you can come back now. Denise is fine, and you have a healthy baby...girl." I turned and looked at my dad and this time he said, "Well, now your life's *really* about to change."

It didn't take long to realize that Dad wasn't talking about girls vs. boys, but about the changes that come with the commitment to parenthood. I was still adjusting and adapting to my role as a husband. Now I would experience the radical adjustment and adaptation required in my role as a father. I quickly learned that the demand was not just to fulfill my responsibility, but to do so with a heart of sacrificial commitment. In time I learned that if you are truly going to love a child, the overriding need is a willingness to give whatever it takes for the sake of that child. And, above and beyond that, to give that child to the Lord. The moment I first held Ashley in my arms, I committed her to God's keeping and His service. Denise and I both prayed, "Lord, we give her back to you. Please use her as a special instrument for your glory."

If you are truly going to love a child, the overriding need is a willingness to give whatever it takes for the sake of that child.

Ashley grew up way too fast for our comfort, but that's how life is. The years were filled with countless activities at home and church and school, punctuated with special moments along the way. When Ashley was two years old, her brother Clint was born, and one year later, Matthew arrived. Each year flew by in a blur of church activities, school projects, slumber parties, track meets, friendships and dating. Before we knew it, Ashley was graduating from high school, and then it was on to nursing school at Samford University and from there to Vanderbilt, where she received her degree as a nurse practitioner.

Commitment carried us through those years—the commitment that Denise and I had for one another, the commitment we shared in raising **We did everything in our power to show commitment in our lives and to call for it in theirs.** Ashley, Clint and Matthew, and above all the commitment of our lives to the lordship of Jesus Christ. Of all the qualities we endeavored to instill in each of our children, depth of commitment was paramount. We did everything in our power to show commitment in our lives and to call for it in theirs. We challenged them to be open and willing to go through any door God opened for them.

Ashley and Matt had both been praying for an out-of-the-box opportunity in international ministry. Both were at transitional points in their lives, out of college and in the workforce but seeking something beyond the mundane. I casually mentioned their desire to a dear friend, Jerry Prevo, and he took the initiative to call our mutual friend, Franklin Graham, president of Samaritan's Purse, the international Christian relief organization. Late that night, about 12:30am, I was startled awake by the phone ringing. "Kirk," he said, "this is Franklin. Hope I'm not calling too late. I heard about your kids and I've had them on my heart. I have a little project I want to invite them to join me on.

The first hand to reach out to people in need should be the hand of Jesus. *We* are that hand.

Could all of you come up here to talk about it?" I told him that I would pass the word first thing in the morning and that I was sure they'd be more than interested. They were, of course, and a couple days later we were all gathered in Franklin's office at the Samaritan's Purse headquarters in North Carolina.

We exchanged pleasantries for a bit and then Franklin turned to Ashley and said, "Sudan is the most desperately needy country in the world. There's been a civil war there for decades, and the U.N. calls it the most dangerous place on earth. We have a field hospital near the Darfur region and we treat people there who have been shot, beaten, slashed with machetes, and tortured by Muslim forces from the north. There's also every kind of disease you can imagine, and if that wasn't bad enough, our hospital has been bombed seven times. These people are going through so much, and I think that when this kind of thing is happening, the first hand to reach out to people in need should be the hand of Jesus. *We* are that hand. Ashley, you're a talented nurse and I want to invite you to join our team at the hospital in Lui."

I don't know if there was any color left in my face after Franklin finished talking, but before I knew it Ashley was answering the invitation. "Mr. Graham," she said, "my daddy trusts you and we've always been taught to live by faith and make strong commitments. I believe God has prepared me for this, so sign me up." I thought, *Sign me up? Doesn't this require a family meeting? No one asked me for a vote.* I looked at Denise, but like me she was speechless and her eyes were so full of tears she probably couldn't see me. I looked back at Ashley and before I could say a word Franklin spoke again. "Matthew," he said, "I want to talk to you about a tougher assignment." I thought, *Tougher assignment? Are you kidding me?* After a momentary pause Franklin continued: "In southern Sudan we have identified more than 200 churches that the radical Muslims have either bombed, burned or looted. In many of the churches they locked the people inside, tied the pastors to the doors and burned them to the ground." He paused again, letting the picture form in our minds. "Son," he said, "I want you to go in and get the names and stories of every pastor that has been killed. I want you to get the names of all the Christians who have been killed and all the churches that have been destroyed. And I want you to commit to leading the effort to build five churches for every one that has been destroyed and to raise up five pastors for every one who has been martyred. Jesus Christ will stand in the end." I looked at Matt and I thought, *This is happening too fast for me*. Matthew's exact words were, "Mr. Graham, I can't let my sister make me look bad. Sign me up, too."

This chain of events was calling us to a new kind of commitment ourselves —a commitment to re-surrender our children to Christ.

On the way back home Ashley and Matt reminded us that we had raised them to look for big challenges and respond with wholehearted commitment. That's exactly what they had done. In our hearts, Denise and I were realizing that this chain of events was calling us to a new kind of commitment ourselves—a commitment to re-surrender our children to Christ, even though they were young adults. A mere three weeks later, Ashley and Matt were in the Sudan, launching full speed into the most extraordinary opportunity of their young lives.

Ashley worked for several indescribably intense months at the hospital in Lui, often experiencing more heart-wrenching moments in a single day than many people experience in a lifetime. Just before Christmas 2005 she was scheduled to return to the U.S. for the holidays when I received a call via satellite phone. I expected that it was Ashley calling to let us know she was on her way home, but it was Matt on the other end of the line. "Dad, Mom, don't ask any questions. Just stop whatever you're doing right now and listen. Ashley's team is under attack at the airstrip in Lui. One is confirmed dead." Then there was a long pause as Matt wept. He continued, "We don't know if it's Ashley. I will call back as soon as I can. I should have been there, I should have been there to protect my sister." He abruptly hung up. It was as if all the air had been sucked out of our lungs. Denise and I immediately got on our faces before God, praying for Ashley and the other team members, not knowing what was going on a world away from us. It was four and a half gruelling hours before we got the call and heard Ashley's beautiful voice on the line. She was still shaken but managed to give us a few of the details.

[Matt] abruptly hung up. It was if all the air had been sucked out of our lungs. Denise and I immediately got on our faces before God, praying for Ashley and the other team members.

Three weeks before Ashley was to leave Sudan to return home for the Christmas holidays, an urgent call came into the hospital requesting aid for a man who had been shot. Ashley and her best friend and fellow nurse Karen Daniels decided to drive to the man's village and attempt to save his life. After a spine-jarring four-hour drive they reached the makeshift hut where he lay writhing in pain. In a region ravaged by decades of war, populated with literally millions of refugees, two young white girls had chosen to go and tend to the wounds of one dying man whom they had never met.

The man, a tribesman of the Dinka Bor, had been shot once in the side, once in the stomach. His eyes were wide with fear, though at last he was getting the help he desperately needed. Michael Abraham was his name, and they guessed him to be about 40 years old. Because of the long-running war, many Sudanese don't know their birthdays and often lose count of their actual age. Ashley and Karen stabilized him, stopped his bleeding and loaded him onto their small truck for the rough journey back to the hospital. Along the way, they were surrounded by the panorama of suffering that is Sudan—countless people, aimlessly wandering, without hope, wondering where their next meal would come from. And everywhere they looked were the evidences of war—bombed and burned structures, and soldiers of the Sudanese Peoples Liberation Army brandishing rifles, machine guns, grenades and RPGs. This was the world they chose to enter willingly, a choice driven by love and commitment to Christ.

Upon arriving back at the hospital, Michael was taken immediately into surgery. His condition, however, continued to deteriorate. When it was apparent that he wasn't going to improve, Ashley and Karen requested governmental permission to transport him to Kenya where he could receive more extensive treatment. The permission was granted and they made plans to take him on the small plane that was scheduled to ferry them to Nairobi. Once in Kenya, Ashley would catch her flight back to the U.S. She and Karen loaded Michael into their truck about 11am in order to get a head start on others who would also be on the flight—Dr. Dick Furman, a surgeon, Scott Hughett, Samaritan's Purse (SP) Special Projects Director, Doug Crockett, SP Director for the Southern Sudan, Gomer Roseman, administrator of the Lui Hospital, and Mel Graham, a businessman and cousin to Franklin Graham.

In a region ravaged by decades of war, populated with millions of refugees, two young girls chose to go and tend to the wounds of one dying man.

A supply truck had departed the hospital about 10 minutes before Ashley and Karen left with their patient. Fifteen minutes behind them was the vehicle carrying the five SP leaders. The first two trucks had arrived at the grass airstrip when the crisis exploded. Karen was in the back of their truck, tending to Michael; Ashley was standing by the liftgate with Maurice, a hospital employee. At that moment a group of men wielding machine guns approached them, feigning friendliness. The leader of the group reached out to shake Ashley's hand but then saw Michael and shouted, "Hey, we want him!" Michael, terrified by the men, clutched Karen's arm as she answered, "No! This is our patient and we have official permission to transport him." In an instant, guns were raised and pointed at all three of them; one soldier grabbed Ashley by the hair and flung her to the ground. She yelled at Maurice to radio the leaders who hadn't yet arrived, but before he had a chance to act the attackers tied him up and began to beat him mercilessly. Two of the soldiers started to struggle with Karen as she used her body to shield Michael from his would-be captors. As the scuffle ensued, the third SP vehicle arrived on the scene; Doug Crockett and Gomer got out and walked into the fray. Ashley shouted to them, "They've beat up our driver...they want Michael!" Her words infuriated the soldier, prompting him to force her head into the ground with his boot.

One soldier grabbed Ashley by the hair and flung her to the ground. She yelled at Maurice to radio the leaders who hadn't yet arrived.

While all this was erupting the SP plane landed and taxied directly toward the scene of madness. Agitated more than ever, the insurgent holding the machine gun to Ashley's head left her on the ground and walked over to the truck. He pulled the pin on a hand grenade and held it menacingly over Karen and Michael. Ashley stood up and watched his every movement. Seeing what he had done she screamed, "He just pulled the pin on the grenade!" The attackers, shouting loudly in Arabic, were in a frenzy. Michael, understanding their threats, began to plead for his life. Karen, still at his side, refused to budge. Ashley walked directly toward the melee, still shouting, "He's pulled the pin on the grenade!" Pulling her back, Gomer said urgently to Ashley, "Get to the plane, now!" She turned and began to walk toward the aircraft and had taken just a few steps when shots rang out. The gunman had put the pin back into the hand grenade and then shot Michael multiple times at point-blank range. "What are you doing! What are you doing!" Karen cried loudly, but the soldiers were unmoved and began to make their way back into the bush. Doug Crockett shouted for everyone to run for the plane. Dr. Furman hurried to the truck and joined Karen in trying to put pressure on the gunshot wounds riddling Michael's body. With all the urgency they could muster, they carried him to the plane, which sat idling on the runway about 100 yards away. On board, Ashley and Karen assisted Dr. Furman, all of them covered with blood. The pilot, fearful of being shot down, was hesitant in taking off; Mel Graham convinced him to do so without delay. As the twin-engine Cessna soared into the sky, gunfire rang out as Islamic insurgents fired wildly at the aircraft. Fortunately, none of the bullets found their mark.

As the twin-engine Cessna soared into the sky, gunfire rang out as Islamic insurgents fired wildly at the aircraft.

In the back of the plane, Dr. Furman pulled a sheet over Michael's lifeless body. They had done all they could do, but he was gone.

The plane made its way safely to Kenya, where Ashley was able to call and let us know what had happened. She had made a commitment, put her life on the line and experienced a crisis of unforgettable intensity. However, even after what she had survived, Ashley talked mainly of her friend, Karen. "What she did was heroic, Dad. She risked her life trying to save Michael. She is an amazing woman."

Ashley is back in the States now, preparing for yet another commitment and a new venture of faith in South America. Matt, of course, is still in the Sudan, living a life of revolutionary commitment that few people ever know. Our other son, Clint, lives in Atlanta and is youth pastor at one of America's most remarkable churches. He is challenging a new generation of teenagers to take up the cross and follow Christ with total commitment to the Savior. Denise and I are deeper than ever into the ministry God has given us, still learning more of what it means to live a radically committed life. We've all been reminded that although only a few of us are called to serve in a place like Sudan, all of us are called to commitment wherever God plants us. This and other experiences have taught me some profound lessons about listening to God, surrendering to his will, committing to his purposes and pressing forward to fulfill the commitments that are made. These are the priorities.

1. Keep listening.

God speaks to us. Through the message of the Word, the counsel of godly people, the evidence of God-directed circumstances and the witness of the Spirit in our hearts, he communicates with us. Unfortunately, we don't always listen. We often get so caught up in listening to our own hearts that we fail to hear the beat of his heart. We are so distracted by the clamor of other things pleading for our attention that

We often get so caught up in listening to our own hearts that we fail to hear the beat of his heart.

we miss his pleadings. This is why, spiritually speaking, we absolutely must keep listening. Otherwise we won't get the wisdom our minds crave and the guidance our hearts require.

This chapter is about commitment, and I am more convinced than ever that it begins with listening. Think back to when you were a child. How often did you get into trouble because you simply didn't listen? For me it was a problem that took a long time to overcome and I sometimes thought of Mom and Dad as a railroad crossing—I had to stop, look and listen or else I might get slammed by an unexpected force! It's like that in the Christian life, too. Failing to stop, look and listen to what God is saying can result in spiritually traumatic consequences.

Here's my counsel: Start your day and end your day with a simple prayer for God to help you listen—to hear all that He is communicating to you, through all the avenues of that communication. If you make it a habit to start and end each day with that petition, you'll begin thinking that way throughout the day as well, and you'll hear more clearly what He wants you to hear. You'll also be better prepared for the second priority...

2. Keep surrendering.

The Christ-life is not lived only on the basis of a one-time commitment. It demands the discipline of constant commitment, constant surrender. There is, of course, a one-time commitment of one's life to Christ in the moment faith is first exercised. However, there's so much more. We could compare it to a marriage in which two people are joined by one public expression of commitment but reaffirmed by countless other expressions of commitment thereafter. The relationship, like the commitment, is dynamic, not static. But it seems that many Christ-followers have gotten the idea that Christianity is like a vaccination— one shot and you're covered for life. In a positional sense that may be true; but in a practical sense it is not.

It seems that many Christ-followers have gotten the idea that Christianity is like a vaccination—one shot and you're covered for life.

I can say that I have surrendered my life to Christ; but I can also truthfully say that I am still surrendering, day by day, moment by moment. There are many synonyms for this spiritual reality—yielding, relying, presenting, and other terms. Paul expressed it like this: "Offer your bodies as living sacrifices, holy and pleasing to God— this is your spiritual act of worship." And then he added, "Do not conform any longer to the pattern of this world, but be transformed by the renewing of your mind. Then you will be able to test and approve what God's will is—his good, pleasing and perfect will."[1] One translation says it like this: "Don't be crammed into the mold of this world." As believers we are only sojourners here, merely passing through this life on our way to another. According to Philippians, "Our citizenship is in heaven. And we eagerly await a Savior from there, the Lord Jesus Christ."[2] For that reason, above all others, we must keep surrendering our will to his will. In doing so, we fulfill the next priority...

3. Keep sacrificing.

A dear friend of mine says, "Sacrifice is giving up something you love for something you love more." He and his wife had already raised several wonderful children and were settling into a new phase of family life when God moved them from the ordinary to the extraordinary. At the time, he was executive pastor of one of America's largest churches. The congregation had just finished a major building project under his direction and he had assembled a strong team to guide that process to a very successful conclusion. After the intensive part of the capital campaign had ended, a group of women from the church asked if they could meet with him. Essentially they had one question: *What is the next big thing we can do?* They wanted a challenge, an assignment. That meeting led to discussions and prayer and ultimately to the decision to

They had one question: *What is the next big thing we can do?* They wanted a challenge, an assignment.

establish a crisis pregnancy center. He assured every-one involved that it would take a true sacrificial com-mitment across the board.

My friend and his wife became very involved in the new project and were overjoyed by the hundreds of young women whose lives were being transformed through the work of the center. For many of them, mostly teenagers, it was the first time they had ever heard reasonable, compelling alternatives to abortion. And in the process, many of those girls chose to receive Christ's gift of eternal life, even as they chose to give their babies the gift of physical life. Through cir-cumstances too complicated to briefly explain, my friends were presented with the opportunity to adopt two babies that one young lady wanted them to raise as their own—babies who otherwise would have been abortion statistics if not for the crisis pregnancy cen-ter. It would have been so easy to say *No*, to keep on with the comfortable life they had settled into, but God moved in their hearts and they embraced those two babies with a sacrificial love. And through it all, the power of commitment made its indelible impact.

Recently I was privileged to have dinner with the legendary basketball coach John Wooden and his daughter. Each of us around the table had a host of questions for him, and I was especially interested in one subject. "Coach," I said, "your players respected you and there's no question that you had a profound influence on their lives long after they left UCLA. How did you use those same principles with your own children, and how did they turn out?" He smiled kindly and turned to his daughter, who is already a woman in her early 70s. "I'll let my daughter answer that question, Kirk." She looked at him with a gleam in her eyes and said something I will never forget. "Daddy has never stopped investing in us and sacrificing for our dreams." What a testimony, and what a revolutionary legacy! I pray daily that I will have the same kind of influence on my own children. And if you are a parent, or if there are people in your life who depend on you, don't stop sacrificing for them. It is one of the most Christ-like and God-honoring of all qualities.

4. Keep committing.

Staying in a state of surrender prepares a Christ-follower to more sensibly make and keep spiritual commitments. A person who is not truly and whole-heartedly surrendered to God cannot make meaningful promises to God. As a pastor I counseled with a number of people who all told me essentially the same thing: "Pastor, I was [in trouble/in debt/in jail/on drugs/at my lowest point/etc.] and I promised God if he got me out of it, I would be a better Christian. He did his part, but I didn't do mine." The problem in all those cases was that promises were made from desperate hearts rather than surrendered hearts.

To make a commitment is to make an agreement; to keep a commitment is to fulfill the agreement, even if circumstances change or difficulties arise. Undoubtedly you've heard reports or read stories of professional athletes who have made contractual commitments to be paid a specific (usually exorbitant) amount of money, later to demand revised contracts paying even more money because they simply feel they're entitled to even more. To them, the commitment is conditional, subject to their own whims and wishes.

In the spiritual realm, commitments are not subject to review and renegotiation.

In the spiritual realm, commitments are not subject to review and renegotiation. In fact, they demand an attitude of affirmation, continually re-committing to the commitment. That's how a marriage works best, and it's certainly how the Christ-life is best lived.

5. Keep pressing.

One of the most inspiring verses in the Bible says, "I press on to take hold of that for which Christ Jesus took hold of me. I do not consider myself yet to have taken hold of it. But one thing I do: Forgetting what is behind and straining toward what is ahead, I press on toward the goal to win the prize for which God has called me heavenward in Christ Jesus."[3]

Life in Christ is not without an aim. We are moving inexorably toward a goal, and that goal is to win the prize for which he has called us heavenward. What is the prize? Is it a crown we can lay at his feet? Is it simply the word of his favor spoken as a loving Father to his children? We actually don't know for sure, but we do know that nothing else in life compares in value to the high priority of pressing forward with full commitment to Christ.

2

Revolutionary Stewardship

Managing the Trust You've Been Given

While scouting locations for a popular TV series, an advance team came upon the perfect site for an action sequence—an impressive house with an expansive, verdant lawn. Unfortunately, the script called for cars to be spinning and crashing on the lawn, tearing out shrubs and mowing down flower beds. But the residents of the south Florida home were so infatuated by the possibility of having their home featured on a prime-time show, they gave their approval on the spot. Days later, the film crew arrived and began shooting. Cars driven by Hollywood stunt drivers were soon careening wildly across the front yard, violently ripping through the turf. That was when a neighbor called the owner of the house—in New York. The scouts had asked the residents for their permission to film, not realizing they were only tenants who had absolutely no authority to allow the property to be harmed, much less destroyed. Understandably, the owner was not a happy man, the director was embarrassed, and the residents were soon looking for a new place to live.

Renters are not owners, they are stewards; and the biggest difference between them can be defined with two words—*rights* and *responsibilities*. Owners have rights. Stewards have responsibilities. It's exactly the same in our relationship with God. He is the owner; we are the stewards. Even our physical bodies belong to him, not to us! We are merely tenants in the flesh and blood God has given us! You don't believe me? Well, here's what the Bible says about the earthly "house" in which we live this life: "Do you not know that your body is a temple of the Holy Spirit, who is in you, whom you have received from God? You are not your own; you were bought at a price. Therefore honor God with your body."[1]

Owners have rights. Stewards have responsibilities. It's exactly the same in our relationship with God.

Stewardship is not a subject that's dry as dust. Far from it. In fact, it holds the potential for revolutionary, transformational power. But tapping into that power demands that we grasp some crucial principles.

Many years ago, when construction began on a proposed bridge across the Niagara River, the first matter at hand was how to span the torrent with the bridge's huge suspension cables. Launching a simple kite, the builders were able to get a thin string across the river. Using the string, they then drew a rope across, which was followed by a larger rope, then a small cable, and finally a cable heavy enough to use as support in building the bridge. When it was completed, the huge structure that could support the heaviest trains gave no hint of having once been launched by a simple kite!

The huge structure that could support the heaviest trains gave no hint of having once been launched by a kite!

I'm reminded by this fascinating, true story that to do a great work you must begin small, and you must keep it simple. This is one of life's foundational facts. Yet the inherent human urge is to make complex what is actually basic. Perhaps that's why churches unnecessarily complicate the matter of stewardship, making burdensome what God intended to be rewarding, fulfilling and even exhilarating. So, concerning stewardship, let's start small and let's keep it simple. Let's grasp those essential principles that undergird our lives— God's timeless truths of stewardship, the indisputable, spiritual laws that must be acknowledged by every believer. Churches in which these truths are taught have more vibrant and expansive ministries. And though these principles are simple, they are not simplistic; and in practicing them we experience spiritually effective lives.

Timeless Truth #1:
God owns everything.

We speak often of "our" possessions, but the basic fact of Scripture is that we actually own nothing. As we've already been reminded, we are stewards of all that God has placed in our trust, but not owners. Our "giving" is, in fact, our management of his resources. The days we live, the positions we fill, the children we nurture, the people we influence, the homes we inhabit, the things we use, the money in our accounts—must all be recognized as belonging to someone else. Of these, the stewardship of money can be the most challenging. Martin Luther astutely observed: "There are three conversions necessary: the conversion of the heart, the mind and the purse. Of these three, it may well be that we find the conversion of the purse most difficult."

Though these principles are simple, they are not simplistic.

The young shepherd David wrote, "The earth is the Lord's, and everything in it."[2] Even earlier in history, Deuteronomy declared: "But you shall remember the Lord your God; for He alone gives you power to get wealth..."[3] Apart from God's grace, we are nothing and have nothing. Yet God chooses to bless us, lovingly allowing us to enjoy and care for so much. But there is no room for self-centered hoarding. As Jesus warned his disciples: "Be on your guard against all kinds of greed, for a man's life does not consist in the abundance of his possessions."[4] He is rightful owner of all things, and real joy comes to us only in acknowledging him and wisely managing his resources.

In North America the prevailing passion is for ownership. We want to own houses, own cars, own investment portfolios, own everything we can get our hands on. But we can easily put ourselves at spiritual risk by getting so focused on this temporal world that we forget to set our affections on things above.[5] The inescapable reality is that "we brought nothing into this world, and it is certain we can carry nothing out."[6] When a billionaire dies, how much does he leave? He leaves it all. All of his earthly riches stay right here, becoming the property of someone else who will also one day abandon them. But there's a way to send riches ahead, to "lay up treasures"[7] in the life that never ends. That's why the wisest stewards are the ones who practice the original, biblical meaning of "paying it forward."

> **The inescapable reality is that "we brought nothing into this world, and it is certain we can carry nothing out."**

Timeless Truth #2:
God's work must be supported by God's people.

In the plan of God, believers are to support the work of God. Biblically, this is expressed in four different types of giving:

REGULAR GIVING, in which God directs his people to give according to a specific, consistent pattern;

RESPONSIVE GIVING, in which God calls upon believers to give in proportion to his blessing upon them;

RELIANT GIVING, in which a commitment to give is based not on what one has but on what one is believing God to supply;

REVELATION GIVING, which occurs when God reveals a specific need and impresses upon the believer to meet it.

Giving is a lifestyle, not an activity; and it emanates from the very character of God, the perfect and eternal Giver. When we give we reflect his life and we show that we are "partakers of the divine nature."[8]

Timeless Truth #3:
God holds every person accountable.

Daniel Webster, the illustrious American statesman, was once asked, "Mr. Webster, what is the most profound thought you have ever had?" He replied, "The most profound and important thought ever to occupy my mind is that I am individually accountable to Almighty God." Webster knew the Scriptures well, especially the truth that each one of us will stand in judgment before the Lord of all creation and give account for how we have lived and how we have managed the assets placed in our care. It is because of that fact that the Bible reminds us, "...it is

> **"The most profound and important thought ever to occupy my mind is that I am individually accountable to Almighty God."**

required of stewards that one be found trustworthy."[9]

Timeless Truth #4:
God's will is that we give wisely and generously.

God is delighted when we give out of a willing and joyful heart. He also desires that we give wisely, investing his resources and not squandering them. I have seen this principle applied in literally hundreds of churches as they have sought God's will in meeting a major need. At such times it is insightful to ask: Is this need proven and spiritual? Does it fit with our mission? Will meeting this need be pleasing to God? Is this the right time to meet the need? Practically speaking, what is the wisest, most effective way to meet this need? I can assure you: God blesses this kind of soul-searching, and what applies to a church is also fitting to us as individual believers.

Timeless Truth #5:
God desires equal commitment,
not equal contribution.

This truth is fundamental to the practice of biblical stewardship in the local church because it under- scores the priority of making the most of what we are given by God. The wealthy per-

To give sacrificially, one must give out of need, not out of abundance.

son who gives a substantial gift may not be giving sacrificially, while the poorer person who makes a far smaller gift may be giving in a radically sacrificial way. To give sacrificially, one must give out of need, not out of abundance. One must *give up* something, not just *give away* something. Jesus taught this lesson when He spoke of the widow who gave two mites (a very small sum of money): "...this poor widow has put in more than all those who have given to the treasury; for they put in out of their abundance, but she out of her poverty put in all that she had, her whole liveli- hood."[10] True sacrifice always results in personal cost to the giver.

Timeless Truth #6:
God holds more responsible
those to whom more is given.

This truth is non-negotiable, and it is crucial to church leaders. As individuals to whom God has given greater position and influence, it is imperative to lead by example as generous, sacrificial givers. There's a vivid example of this kind of leadership in the life of David when he publicly led the way in giving. "Moreover," he said, "I have set my affections on the house of my God, I have given to the house of my God, over and above all that I have prepared for the holy house, my own special treasure of gold and silver."[11] David gave "over and above" his already substantial offerings. He gave from his special treasure, clearly a resource he prized very highly. In response to his leadership, others followed and "offered willingly" to the building of the temple. The final result recorded is that "the people rejoiced" as they gave out of grateful, loyal hearts.

Timeless Truth #7:
God blesses the giver in proportionate measure.

God does not need anything; yet, mysteriously, he wants us to grow in grace by giving to him. As we obey him in practicing this spiritual discipline, he blesses us accordingly. Jesus said, "Give, and it will be given to you; good measure, pressed down, shaken together, running over, they will pour into your lap. For by your standard of measure it will be measured to you in return."[12]

Notice that the full title of this chapter is:

Revolutionary Stewardship
Managing the Trust You've Been Given

Whether you're aware of it or not, you are the manager of a trust. You have been given a key role and a great responsibility, and it is imperative to make the most of it. The God of the universe has entrusted you with time, money, material things and great opportunities. Your objective is to maximize the investment of all that he has put into your hands. Every day is a new opportunity for service and stewardship. Time is a precious commodity and we have a limited allotment of days, hours and minutes. In light of that, the Scriptures advise us, "Be very careful, then, how you live—not as unwise but as wise, making the most of every opportunity."[13] In the context of true stewardship, money is a means to an end, not the end itself. There's no getting around the fact that the allure of money is strong and pervasive. It permeates our entire, obsessive culture; but it brings no lasting fulfillment. It always creates a thirst for

Your objective is to maximize the investment of all that he has put into your hands.

more, unless one has the right attitude toward it and determines to manage it rather than be manipulated by it. In the final analysis, the hallmark of stewardship is wise management with the motive of pleasing the true owner.

One of my elementary school teachers used to say, "The best ability is dependability." It sounded corny to me back then, but I now realize how relevant that adage is in the realm of stewardship. Paul wrote to the Corinthians: "Now it is required that those who have been given a trust must prove faithful."[14] The Phillips translation puts it this way: "Now what we look for in stewards is that they should be trustworthy." Trustworthiness, faithfulness, dependability—whatever word you use, the point is the same: God wants us to be people he can count on, people who live with a servant's heart. Jesus once told his disciples, "You know that those who are regarded as rulers of the Gentiles lord it over them, and their high officials exercise authority over them. Not so with you. Instead, whoever wants to become great among you must be your servant, and whoever wants to be first must be slave of all. For even the Son of Man did not come to be served, but to serve, and to give his life as a ransom for many."[15] At the most basic level, the true steward is a true servant.

Faithful dependability as a Christian steward

relates to the management of money, but also to a great deal more. The "portfolio" for which we are responsible includes a wide range of "assets", and God's expectation is that we make the most of each one. Think of all that you have under management: your money, your time, your possessions, your opportunities, your influence, your relationships and more. And to this long list can be added the spiritual assets with which we are entrusted: the Gospel of Christ, the mystery of godliness, the secret things of God. This is no small responsibility we bear, and to handle it rightly demands absolute faithfulness.

The "portfolio" for which we are responsible includes a wide range of assets.

In just about every one of Paul's epistles there is a clear statement about the priority of faithfulness. In the very first verse of Ephesians, he addresses "the saints in Ephesus, the faithful in Christ Jesus."[16] At the outset of Colossians, he writes, "To the holy and faithful brothers in Christ at Colosse."[17] To his spiritual son, Timothy, he repeatedly reinforced this same truth. And throughout the Bible we see that faithfulness is essential to serving God, to declaring his Word, to helping other believers and to handling situations of responsibility. From the Old Testament straight through the New, the wise, effective steward is shown to be utterly faithful. We see this virtue in Joseph when he was unjustly imprisoned. We observe it in Moses as he managed an entire nation in the middle of a wasteland. We find it in Daniel, who ran a government and could not be put down by his enemies, for "they could find no corruption in him, because he was trustworthy."[18] We see it in men like Epaphras whom Paul called "our dear fellow servant, who is a faithful minister of Christ."[19]

Here's the bottom line: To be a trustworthy steward, you must see everything in life as sacred. For the believer, everything in life *is* sacred, and everything is to be devoted to the Lord. Whatever your treasures, whatever your talents, dedicate them to God's purpose. "Whatever you do, do it all for the glory of God."[20]

3

Revolutionary Servanthood

Paying the Price of Service

Jesus Christ has often been called a revolutionary. Not because he led a revolt or took over a government or wrote a book that sparked a great rebellion. He was a completely different kind of revolutionary, one whose very presence on earth was unique among men, the dividing line in human history and in human hearts. The things Jesus said about himself were without question revolutionary statements. He made claims that, if they were not true, would put him in the category of a madman or an outrageous fabricator. What Jesus said was astonishing...

> *"I and the Father are one."* [1]

> *"If you have seen me, you have seen the Father."* [2]

> *"I am the way the truth and the life. No one comes to the Father except through me."* [3]

He did not present himself as *a* way, but *The* Way. He did not claim to *know* God, but to *be* God. And, as C. S. Lewis wrote, the nature of his assertions demand that he be seen either as a liar, a lunatic, or as the Lord of all creation. There is really no middle ground when it comes to one's view of Christ. Either you are with him or against him. Either you have put your faith in him alone or you're putting your faith in someone or something else. In an age of such spongy, easy-believism, with tolerance elevated to the status of virtue, the claims of Christ are like ice water splashed in the face of convention. To those who say that all religions lead to God, that all beliefs are equally valid, I calmly but firmly say, "That's not what Jesus said, and that's not what the Bible teaches." The very first followers of Christ, the disciples who encountered the resurrected Lord and saw him ascend back into the heavens, were not bashful nor hesitating in their witness. "Salvation is found in no one else," they said, "for there is no name under heaven given to men by which we must be saved."[4] *Only in Jesus, only through Him*. That was the message they declared and kept declaring, even though many were executed for saying it.

He did not present himself as *a* way, but *The* Way. He did not claim to *know* God, but to *be* God.

I make no apologies for believing Jesus Christ to be exactly who he said he was: God, Savior, Lord. Long ago I crossed the line of faith and put my trust in him, receiving the gift he offers to all who come—the gift of eternal life. And I believe that the life he gives begins right here and now, and that it continues into the life to come. I take the apostle Paul's words to heart: "If in this life alone we have hope in Christ we are of all people most miserable."[5] Well, I'm not miserable because I know that the hope is forever.

The question I face daily as a believer (as do all Christ-followers) is this: How do I best live for Christ right now? How do I follow his example and live a spiritually revolutionary life today? The answer, I am convinced, is found in looking at

How do I best live for Christ right now? How do I follow his example and live a spiritually revolutionary life today?

the most revolutionary thing Jesus did—becoming not just a human being, but a lowly servant. The God of all lowered himself to become nothing, and then further humbled himself to die a sacrificial death on a roughly-hewn cross. The thought of it is still beyond my feeble, finite comprehension, but I believe it, accept it and I am continually changed by it. And in looking at him, the servant Christ, I see the mindset that must permeate all that I do. Philippians 2:5-8 describes it so eloquently:

*Your attitude should be the same
as that of Christ Jesus: Who,
being in very nature God, did not
consider equality with God something to be grasped, but made
himself nothing, taking the very
nature of a servant, being made in
human likeness. And being found
in appearance as a man, he humbled himself and became obedient
to death—even death on a cross!*

We are called to a life of revolutionary servanthood. It is counter to our human nature, of course. We want to be served, not to serve. We want to receive, not to give. That's just the way we're wired as human beings; but Christ calls us to something higher, although it is reached by lowering ourselves just as he humbled himself for us. The 12 disciples whom Jesus called were just like us. They argued about who was greater, who would be closest to the Master, who would get the most recognition. But he told them, "the first shall be last, and the last shall be first" and "he who humbles himself will be exalted."[6] The natural urge is against being a servant; but Christ in us gives the power to overcome that urge and live like he lived.

Let me share with you five important motivations for revolutionary servanthood.

We serve because we're forgiven.

One of my colleagues recently received a highly unusual request. A dying man contacted him and asked, "Could you come visit me in the hospital? I want you to tell me about God." That simple request jarred my friend; his human nature was instantly saying *No* to the request; but Christ in his heart was saying *Yes*. Fortunately, the words came out, "Yes, I'll come see you." The reason for the inner turmoil is understandable. My colleague explained, "The man who was asking me to come see him was the man who had an affair with my wife and caused our marriage to break up. They subsequently married and divorced also, but the pain still haunts me. It's like the ghost of an old injury." He went on to tell me, "Whenever I thought of that man, I remembered that he was the reason my kids had to shuttle between two homes. He was the cause of tremendous grief. So here he was dying of lung cancer, days from a godless eternity, asking me of all people to help him." As I listened to my friend, I thought, *How would I handle such a situation? What would I do?* His story continued, "At first, I didn't know if I could follow through with it, but then I remembered that it wasn't about me and what I wanted; it was

So here he was dying of lung cancer, days from a godless eternity, asking me of all people to help him."

about God and what he desired from me as a servant of Christ. I went to the hospital with the love of Jesus in my heart and I told that man the Good News that he could receive the gift of salvation if he put his faith in Christ alone. With a lot of emotion and tears of joy he opened his heart and prayed to receive God's forgiveness. He died three weeks later, but I was told he spent those last weeks of his life joyfully telling everybody about his new-found faith."

When I heard that amazing story, I thought, Now that is revolutionary servanthood! Going to someone who has nothing to offer you, someone who has actually hurt you, and sharing with them the message of Christ. I knew that my friend was able to forgive because he had been forgiven, and that is a powerful motivation to Christian service.

Think back once again to those first disciples. After the resurrection, a group of women including Mary Magdalene, Joanna, and Mary the mother of James heard the angel's declaration that the Lord had risen from the dead. They rushed from the empty tomb to tell the apostles. At first the men didn't believe the reports of the women. "Jesus is alive," they said. The disciples were troubled, filled with doubt. Then, one by one, they met him, recognized him, fell at his feet, and worshiped him. He was alive! Hope was reborn!

But what about the past? Would he remember

how they had deserted him...how they had cut and run at the moment of danger? How could they have been so faithless and unbelieving? Jesus quietly reaffirmed his love for them, neither upbraiding them or accusing them. In the days following he spent time among them on several occasions. He allowed them to touch his hands and his side, to settle their doubts and be convinced of his reality. He helped them in their daily needs: directing them to the location of fish when they had caught nothing and fixing them breakfast on the shore. He opened their eyes to the Scriptures. He gave them the promise of his Spirit, to be with them forever. And then, he gave them a mission.

Jesus quietly reaffirmed his love for them, neither upbraiding them or accusing them.

When the disciples were renewed in faith and secure again in his love, he gave them a charge. Those who had so glaringly failed him in his moment of trial were entrusted with the greatest work the world would ever know: the spreading of the Gospel. The past didn't sabotage the present or the future. Their failures would always be a reminder of the weakness of the flesh and the power of sin, but they would not be a barrier to further usefulness. These men, renewed by love and mercy, became revolutionary servants who went on to turn the world upside down.

When we look back at all God has done for us, our hearts should be filled with gratitude for the Lord's goodness. He has always been faithful and forgiving! And, like our counterparts in the first century, we have a mission to carry his truth to our community and to regions beyond. The spiritual revolution continues!

We serve because we're blessed.

There are two seas in the Holy Land. The northern sea, called the Sea of Galilee, is one of the land's most beautiful features. Fed by the Jordan River, it irrigates fertile valleys and helps produce a bounty of fruits and vegetables. Fishermen still ply its depths, finding sustenance and profit. This is the sea that Jesus loved. He knew its waters in stillness and in storm. Upon its banks he taught many parables, spent many nights, and worked his miracles of love and compassion.

The southern sea, further down the Jordan River, differs greatly from Galilee. Its air is filled with the stench of debris and filth. No man or beast will drink from its bitter waters. No children play along its polluted shores. It is a lifeless sea. Its very name reveals its nature: The Dead Sea.

Both seas are fed by the same river. But why the stark difference? It's because the Dead Sea has an inlet to receive the fresh waters, but no outlet to send them on. The fresh waters pour in...only to stagnate and decay.

You can probably think of many people who are just like the Dead Sea. They are utterly self-centered, thinking only of getting more and more for themselves—much like the man in the parable who sought to build bigger barns to protect his increase, never realizing the true nature of his riches. That is the antithesis of Christian service.

The challenge of revolutionary servanthood is to be a "Galilee Christian"—giving out as freely and readily as we take in. Only by living in this way will we be as healthy and joyous as God desires us to be. As Proverbs teaches, "A generous man will prosper; he who refreshes others will himself be refreshed."[7] As we serve wholeheartedly, giving freely and generously of all that we have and all that we are, we extend Christ's Kingdom. We become living examples of the living Word, and we discover the joy of the Galilee principle.

> **The challenge of revolutionary servanthood is to be a "Galilee Christian"— giving out as freely and readily as we take in.**

What is God calling you to do in revolutionary service to him today?

We serve because we're free.

Just a few yards from the gravesite of President Ronald Reagan stands a remarkable monument to freedom—a panel of reinforced concrete that soars to a height of 12 feet. On one side it is covered with festive graffiti, colorful and vibrant; on the other side it is gray and pitted, marked only by a single, letter E spray-painted in black. As a huge chunk of concrete it would have no value except for where it once stood and what it symbolized. For decades it was one panel among thousands in the infamous Berlin Wall, the same wall that President Reagan had called upon Soviet leader Gorbachev to tear down. Today it is a poignant reminder of freedom's high cost and inestimable value.

Freedom in all its forms is a wonderful thing, and true spiritual freedom is the most precious of all, the one that cannot be silenced, neutralized or diminished by any human power. In Christ, God has blessed us with this freedom, liberating us from the death penalty of sin and its power over us. But freedom is a privilege to be rightly exercised, and this leads us directly to one of the paradoxes of the Christian life: We are slaves, yet we're free. The New Testament Greek term translated "servant" is *doulos*, which is more accurately rendered as *slave*. Christ came not only as a servant, but as the lowest form of servant, as a slave. As God in the flesh, Jesus was free to do whatever he wanted, yet he chose to subject his will to the Father's will, surrendering his freedom in order to secure ours.

God has given to each one of us the power to

choose, and an awesome power it is. He doesn't coerce us into his service; he calls us. And when we answer that call, when we pattern our service after his example, it has a revolutionary impact upon us and upon those whom we serve. Energized by his power we become agents of his love and grace.

We serve because we're joyful.

I've been to a lot of prisons. Not as an inmate, fortunately, but as a minister of the Gospel. They're not pretty places, but prisons today are like resorts compared to those in which the apostle Paul languished. He didn't have a heated cell with a private toilet and sink. There was no mattress for sleeping, no TV room for relaxing, no well-stocked library for reading and study. There was only the dark encasement of damp stone walls, a place filled with putrid odors and the pungent reminders of human depravity. Perhaps worst of all were the chains, their rusty coarseness scraping his skin raw, constantly tugging at him.

God doesn't coerce us into his service; he calls us.

And, as if imprisonment were not painful enough, Paul had to endure something worse: the stinging criticism of those who called themselves his Christian brothers. They dared to attack God's messenger even while he was held captive.

Put yourself into Paul's situation. Feel the weight of the chains on raw skin. Taste the nauseating swill that was his daily food. Listen to those dreadful sounds of suffering that filled his ears day and night. Look into the menacing eyes of the Roman prison guards. You are there. You are suffering. You are chained. You are Paul the apostle. Now, what's your attitude? What fills your heart through the weary hours? Here's what Paul wrote to his friends in Philippi:

"Now I want you to know, brothers, that what has happened to me has really served to advance the gospel. As a result, it has become clear throughout the whole palace guard and to everyone else that I am in chains for Christ. Because of my chains, most of the brothers in the Lord have been encouraged to speak the word of God more courageously and fearlessly."[8]

Rather than living in or through the circumstances, he rose above them.

What an attitude! Instead of being inflamed with self-pity, Paul was encouraged by the positive impact of his negative condition. In spite of the severity, he was joyful. What a revolutionary lesson Paul teaches us! We have troubles and trials, sure; but what is our attitude, and what is our commitment? Paul was joyful and he kept on serving; rather than living in or through the circumstances, he rose above them.

We serve because we're loved.

There is much that I enjoy about contemporary Christian music, but I hope we never lose touch with the great hymns. In so many of them there is a richness of expression that is so far removed from today's use of the English language. But it isn't just the deep lyrics that capture my attention; it's the stories that produced those lyrics in the first place. One of the most touching examples is the hymn, "O Love That Will Not Let Me Go" by George Matheson. If you're a young Christian or a new believer, chances are you've never heard it; but I can assure you it came from a heart that understood the meaning of the words.

O Love that wilt not let me go,
I rest my weary soul in thee;
I give thee back the life I owe,
That in thine ocean depths its flow
May richer, fuller be.

O light that followest all my way,
I yield my flickering torch to thee;
My heart restores its borrowed ray,
That in thy sunshine's blaze its day
May brighter, fairer be.

O Joy that seekest me through pain,
I cannot close my heart to thee;
I trace the rainbow through the rain,

And feel the promise is not vain,
That morn shall tearless be.

O Cross that liftest up my head,
I dare not ask to fly from thee;
I lay in dust life's glory dead,
And from the ground there blossoms red
Life that shall endless be.

In the mid-19th century Matheson was a young seminary student in Scotland when he began to go blind. At the time he was engaged to a young lady whom he loved deeply; but when he told her of his deteriorating eyesight his fiancee gave back the engagement ring and told him she simply could not be married to a blind man. Being a blind man in a generation that was unkind to the disabled, George needed someone to provide constant assistance; for years that person was his beloved sister. But she, too, fell in love and was soon engaged. It was on the night of her wedding that Matheson wrote his famous hymn. He described the experience in his diary many years later:

In the manse of Innelan on the evening
of the 6th of June, 1882, I was alone in
the manse at that time. It was the night
of my sister's marriage, and the rest of
the family were staying over night in
Glasgow. Something happened to me,
which was known only to myself, and

which caused me the most severe mental suffering. The hymn was the fruit of that suffering. It was the quickest bit of work I ever did in my life. I had the impression of having it dictated to me by some inward voice rather than of working it out myself. I am quite sure that the whole work was completed in five minutes, and equally sure that it never received at my hands any retouching or correction. I have no natural gift of rhythm. All the other verses I have ever written are manufactured articles; this came like a dayspring from on high.

His eyesight had left him, his fiancee had left him, his sister had left him, and George Matheson was left alone and depressed. But into the depths of that darkness of soul God sent the light of his compassion. George was reminded more poignantly than ever of the love that would never let him go. He was able to "trace the rainbow through the rain"—the vivid reality of hope in Christ.

He was able to "trace the rainbow through the rain"—the vivid reality of hope in Christ.

"O Love That Will Not Let Me Go" became one of the most widely sung hymns of its era, perhaps because so many people could identify with the personal nature of its promise. George Matheson never married, but he became one of Scotland's leading pastors, often preaching to a congregation of more than 1,500 worshippers. In spite of his handicap, Matheson became known as a friend to the friendless, a man who touched thousands of lives. God had taught him in an unforgettable way the truths of revolutionary servanthood.

4

Revolutionary Contribution

Putting Your Money Where Your Heart Is

You've heard it countless times: "Put your money where your mouth is." Or as someone has paraphrased, "Back up what you say with what you pay." Jesus had an even deeper perspective. He said: "Store up for yourselves treasures in heaven, where moth and rust do not destroy, and where thieves do not break in and steal. For where your treasure is, there your heart will be also."[1] In other words, put your money where your heart is, but make sure your heart is in the right place.

One day near the great Temple of Jerusalem Jesus sat down across from the collection area and watched intently as the offerings were given. People from all walks of life were entering the courtyard to make their contributions to the temple treasury. Among the crowd were a number of rich people who threw in large amounts of money. Undoubtedly some gave with a flourish that drew attention to their great generosity. But then he spotted a lowly widow who entered humbly and put in two very small copper coins, worth only a fraction of a penny. Calling his disciples to him, Jesus said, "I tell you the truth, this poor widow has put more into the treasury than all the others. They gave out of their wealth; but she, out of her poverty, put in everything—all she had to live on."[2]

In one simple act she demonstrated true sacrifice, proven not just by what she had put in, but by what she had left over.

Everyone else had given out of their abundance, but she gave her all. In one simple act she demonstrated true sacrifice, proven not just by what she had put in, but by what she had left over. Her revolutionary contribution showed that the most significant gifts are often given by the most insignificant givers. It's doubtful that anyone but Jesus actually noticed her that day, but God is paying attention and he sees things no one else sees and interprets meaning no one else grasps. What matters to him is wholehearted devotion, and what pleases him is the exercise of genuine faith. The poor widow was wholly devoted to God, willing by faith to give everything. She loved the Lord with an absolute love, and he would bless her for that devotion to him.

Giving to Advance Christ's Kingdom

I have been so encouraged in seeing people today who are just like that widow of ancient days. In our ministry of consulting with churches across the nation we meet some remarkable people, and they're often the least likely to draw one's attention. Take the case of José, a man of little means but great heart. He is a member of a church with whom we partner in Huntington Beach, CA—a church that is making a true spiritual impact upon its community. The church has had such an influx of new people that a larger facility became absolutely essential. José was touched by the need, but he makes minimum wage, uses public transportation and after his tithe barely manages to make ends meet. He told his wife one day, "Honey, I really want us to give more than we're able to give right now. We need to do something extra to help build the new church." They prayed together, asking God to provide a way. The next day José came across an ad in the local paper that caught his attention. A company directly across the street from his regular job was advertising to hire a security guard for the shift from 4:30 to 8:30am. José would be able to go from one job right to the other. He went and applied and was hired immediately. José and his wife are giving literally every penny he makes on that second job to help the church finish its much-needed worship center.

Many people in that congregation can and do give large sums of money to the ministry there, but I wonder if anyone is making a more revolutionary contribution than José in helping to advance the cause of Christ. I look at him and ask myself, *What motivates me to give money for the work of God?* No one helped me to answer that question better than a remarkable woman named Rita.

Giving to Rescue the Perishing

Rita came to our church at the death of her husband, Stanley. I will never forget the first sight of her, alone and broken at that funeral. I did my best to give her comfort and encouragement. Denise and I invited her to our home for dinner that night and she talked on and on about her beloved husband. Our kids were small at the time and they seemed fascinated with her, an elderly but beautiful lady. She and Stanley had spent many years together and all they had was each other; no children, no extended family. She started coming to church and within a few weeks she gave her heart to the Lord.

Over the years that followed Rita prayed for me so fervently. She called my office almost every day with her regular request, "Pastor, how can I pray for you today?" She became a faithful steward and when we faced the greatest capital challenge in our church's history, Rita made an extraordinary financial commitment. She called me one day and said, "Pastor, can I take you to lunch? I want to give you something." There was an urgency in her voice and I sensed it was important to make the time for her, even in the midst of a very busy season. Rita was in her mid-80s by then and had become like a grandmother to me. I picked her up and we drove to her favorite cafe and were seated at her favorite table. It was a noisy place, the clanging of plates and silverware ringing in the air and the din of conversations on all sides. I looked at her and saw that her eyes were filling with tears. Her lips were quivering and she was fighting to keep her emotions in check.

There was an urgency in her voice and I sensed it was important to make the time for her, even in the midst of a very busy season.

"Rita, are you OK?" I asked. "I'm OK, pastor, but I want to give my commitment to the building campaign." She opened up one of those seashell-covered Florida purses and took out a check that was neatly folded in half. She pushed it across the table. I thanked her, pushed it back and said, "Rita, it's not time to make the commitments, and I prefer not to take offerings people give to the church." She gave me a stern grandmotherly look and pushed it back, and when I put my hand on it again, she put hers on top of mine and held it in place. "Pastor," she said forcefully, "it's time for *my* commitment. God has told me in my heart that it's time to give now." I looked at her and asked again, "Rita, are you alright?" She said, "Pastor, have I told you about my Stanley?" I replied, "Oh Rita, you've told me so many of those stories." She looked at me with great seriousness. "Pastor, I'm not sure I will ever see that new church built. I want you to remember something. When you stand up in that new church to preach, somebody just like Stanley might be sitting out there listening to you. Tell him how to know Jesus! Pastor, I will never see Stanley again. We're going to spend eternity in different places!" She wept aloud and I did all I could to comfort her once again.

"When you stand up in that new church to preach, somebody just like Stanley might be sitting out there listening to you. Tell him how to know Jesus!"

When I got back to the office I gave the check to our treasurer. I had intentionally not looked at it, but I knew that regardless of the amount, it was the biggest gift that anyone would contribute to that building campaign. It was Rita's expression of love for the Lord and her passion for others to have a destiny different from her Stanley. Rita is now in heaven, and God has wiped away all her tears; and when I think of her I'm reminded anew that our gifts are so much more than a nice thing to do. They are vital! They are life-changing!

Giving to Meet the World's Greatest Needs

The more I see the needs of people in this world the more I am compelled to give every dollar I can give in the name of Jesus. Recently I came across a mini-essay that speaks with eloquence and conviction to every believer. The author is unknown, but to whomever the writer may be, I am grateful for the admonition. Think on these things...

Can we, who have so much, be touched by those who have so little? Can full stomachs hear the hollow echo of the empty? Can a people drunk on personal freedom, human rights and civil rights, adequately understand those who are held by famine and hunger? Can we who are held captive by our gadgets, entertained by TV, seduced by Hollywood, victimized by our own success, be touched by those who search frantically for individual grains of rice to fill their now-empty bowls? Can we, whose ears are in tune with sound by Pioneer, Sony or Panasonic, hear the plaintive cries of the child in San Paulo, the wailings of a young mother standing above a freshly dug grave in India, or the broken sobs of a father just recently bereaved to

raise six kids in San Salvador? Actually,
who are the deaf, the blind, the crippled,
the hungry? We are! You and I! We have
eyes that cannot see, hearts that cannot
feel, ears that cannot hear, hands that
cannot move and a hunger that cannot
be satisfied! But it is not too late. We can
change! We can alter the charted course
of the starving, empty, lonely peoples of
our world. We must begin immediately.
We must begin now! God help us to
have a growing sensitivity to those
around us. May he open our hearts, our
eyes and our hands on behalf of a hurt-
ing world.

This world is gripped with mind-numbing needs, and it is so easy to look the other way, to turn a deaf ear to the clamor for help. But Christ calls us to look and listen and respond with genuine concern, to give all that we can to accomplish his purposes. It happens, for the most part, one person at a time. You may not be able to feed an entire starving village, rescue thousands of abandoned and orphaned children, or provide shelter for a huddled mass of refugees. But you could feed one person, rescue one child, give shelter to one family. There were times in Jesus' ministry when he fed the multitudes, but mostly we see him touching one life at a time with his miraculous power. By his grace and with his enablement we, too, can touch lives as we make revolutionary contributions for his sake.

Giving to Change a County for Christ

Recently I witnessed firsthand one of the most remarkable examples of revolutionary contribution. Ironically, it happened in the poorest place in all of America—a small town in a small county in the heart of the Appalachian Mountains of West Virginia. Wyoming County is home to approximately 24,000 people. Its principal town, Oceana, has fewer than 2,000 residents. When Jay Morgan came to Oceana in April, 2001 to become pastor of New Life Community Church the future looked grim. The church was a divided congregation of just 20 people, inwardly-focused and discouraged. From day one, Jay determined that he would challenge them to look beyond themselves, to believe God for a great vision, and to begin to serve Christ in every way possible.

There were times in Jesus' ministry when he fed the multitudes, but mostly we see him touching one life at a time.

It took some persistence, but soon there was truly new life at New Life. A handful of members began to reach out to the community and the church began to grow. In a county where the average congregation numbers fewer than 30, New Life grew to 10 times that size. The growth presented a new challenge: where are we going to put all these people? It was clear that something had to give, and Jay knew that it was the people of his flock who had to give. Like the Macedonian believers described in the New Testament, they were poor and disenfranchised, but somehow they had to believe God for a miracle. Bear in mind, Wyoming County is a place of desperate poverty—economically, socially and spiritually. The unemployment rate exceeds 30%. Teen pregnancy is high and alcohol and drug abuse is rampant. Law enforcement officials estimate that at least 65% of the county's adults abuse alcohol and other drugs.

They were poor and dis- enfranchised, but some- how they had to believe God for a miracle.

To address the extreme needs, New Life started after-school programs for children and teens. They organized the county's only drug and alcohol recovery support groups. And they launched a leadership development initiative to break the cycle of victimhood. Space was needed for all of those outreaches, in addition to the burgeoning worship services and Bible classes. Jay, along with Mike Moore and George Smith, two of the church's elders (actually, the only elders at that time), determined that they needed at least $500,000 to build a suitable facility. Half a million dollars. A sum that no church in those rugged hills of Appalachia had ever raised. It would take the revolutionary contribution of God's people, and it began with the fire burning in the hearts of those three young men—Jay Morgan, Mike Moore and George Smith.

I met Jay, Mike and George right after they had determined what it would cost to fund the next phase of their dream. They came to ask for my help in climbing the mountain that loomed before them. Jay said, "We are not going to live in fear and defeat any longer in our county. We are 100% committed to making this happen because if we don't do it, there is no Plan B for the children and the suffering people of our county. It's us or 'lights out.'" I

"If we don't do it, there is no Plan B for the children and suffering people of our county. It's us or 'lights out.'"

admired their tenacity and I knew their faith was real. We promised to do everything possible to be their partner all the way to victory. Prayerfully and strategically, we laid out a plan, and they began to call on the church to give with sacrificial generosity.

On New Life's Commitment Sunday, virtually every person in the church family participated, and what a celebration it was when over $550,000 in pledges were turned in! And, on top of that, cash gifts of $50,000 filled the offering plates. "This really has been revolutionary," Jay told me recently. "The offerings have not just built a building. They have built lives and families, and they have strengthened our entire community."

Giving to Make a Difference

Before I leave the story of New Life Church, let me tell you about Mike Moore, one of those three young leaders. Mike grew up in the area, but he left there some 20 years ago to attend West Virginia University. He graduated with honors and went on to dental school, where he also excelled. Mike met his wife Michelle there and upon finishing their studies the whole world lay ahead of them. They were talented young dentists who could have gone anywhere in the U.S. to set up a lucrative practice. They are very bright, very capable. But when they began to think about how to launch their careers together, they felt compelled to go back to Michelle's hometown of Oceana. There was no question of need. Mike and Michelle would be among just a handful of dentists serving the entire region. They were desperately needed, but the pay would be abysmally less than they could earn anywhere else. They both had the same thought: they wanted to make a difference among the people of Appalachia. But, at the time, they were both far from God.

It wasn't long after their arrival in Oceana that New

Life Church made a huge spiritual impact upon Mike and Michelle. They fully committed their lives to Jesus Christ. The impact that this fine couple have made upon their community cannot be measured in dollars and cents but in lives influenced for the cause of Christ. Their willingness to contribute their significant skills in a place that is so downtrodden and poverty-impaired has infused hope into many hearts. It has also opened up for them innumerable opportunities to share their faith in Christ. As leaders in their community and in New Life Church they are living examples of what it means to give in a way that truly makes a difference.

> **Their willingness to contribute their significant skills in a place that is so downtrodden and poverty-impaired has infused hope into many hearts.**

No one was more influenced by their commitment to Christ than Michelle's father. Dorn Brown was a rough, gruff country guy. He had never attended church, always complaining that he had been turned off by religious people early in his life. He was as far away from God as a man could be. But Dorn was a hard worker, averaging 100 hours a week all his life, most of them in the recesses of a coal mine. When grandchildren arrived, his heart began to soften; but he still didn't want to talk about God. Eventually, as he observed the transformation in Mike and Michelle, and as he saw his grandchildren express love for God, the hard exterior began to crumble.

One day recently Dorn was diagnosed with black lung disease and lung cancer, so common to men who spend their lives in the mines. When his condition worsened, an ambulance was called to take him to a larger hospital in another city. Dorn Brown asked that they hold the ambulance; he called Jay Morgan and Mike Moore to come see him. They arrived and climbed up into the ambulance and in the next few minutes Mike had the opportunity to lead his father-in-law to faith in Christ. Five months later Dorn stepped into eternity, ready to meet God. On his journey to faith the first mile marker was a decision by his loving daughter and son-in-law, a decision to make a revolution-ary contribution. It changed their lives, it made the dif-ference for Dorn Brown, and it is still being used by God in a transformational way.

On his journey to faith the first mile marker was a decision by his loving daughter and son-in-law.

Giving to God What Belongs to God

His enemies wanted desperately to entrap him with his own words. Jesus had rattled them to the core and they were fed up with it. Surely there was some way of getting him to say something blatantly wrong. Surely they could corner him in a situation with no way out. Perhaps they could trick him into taking sides between the religious authorities and the governmental rulers. Yes, that would work. He had to fall for that.

A carefully chosen group was assigned the treacherous task: Go to Jesus, butter him up with a few choice words, then trip him up with the no-win question. With smiles on their faces and evil in their hearts, they approached him. "Teacher," they said, "we know that you are a man of integrity and that you teach the way of God in accordance with the truth. You aren't swayed by men, because you pay no attention to who they are."[3]

Flattery, they were certain, would work on him as it did with everyone else. It was time for the question. They asked him: "Tell us then, what is your opinion? Is it right to pay taxes to Caesar or not?"[4]

Jesus, of course, was not misled at all by their conniving tactics. Knowing their intent, he said, "You hypocrites, why are you trying to trap me? Show me the coin used for paying the tax."[5] He didn't just cut to the chase, he cut right to the heart; and he was about to teach a powerful lesson about giving. They complied with his demand and brought him a denarius, the well-known Roman coin. He asked them, "Whose portrait is this? And whose inscription?"[6]

"Caesar's,"[7] they replied.

With their own answer still ringing in their ears, Jesus then said, "Give to Caesar what is Caesar's, and to God what is God's."[8]

They were stunned. And they were the ones trapped by the question and condemned by the answer. The image and inscription were an indication of ownership, and it could not be argued that a coin minted by Caesar, impressed with his image and embossed with his words would belong to anyone else. "Give to Caesar what is Caesar's," Jesus said, and they could not dispute his logic. But he didn't leave it at that. The lesson wasn't complete, because the most important point was what followed: "Give to God what is God's."[9]

Our very reason for being is to reflect his likeness as he conforms us to himself. We are God's currency.

This life-defining truth is all too often missed, possibly because we're so delighted by the clever way in which Jesus put down the deceivers. But we must not miss his underlying point: Just as Caesar's image and inscription were on that coin, God's image and inscription are on us. We are made in his image and inscribed with his truth. Our very reason for being is to reflect his likeness as he conforms us to himself. We are God's currency.

No truth of stewardship is more basic, yet none is more potent. Giving to God what is God's, first and foremost, means contributing our money, our time, our resources, our very lives unreservedly in his service and for his purposes.

5

Revolutionary Witness

Giving Away Your Faith

On the morning of May 9, 1980, a fierce rain squall swept across Tampa Bay in the straits between St. Petersburg and Bradenton, Florida. A lethal combination of high winds and impossibly thick fog created havoc in the sea. Navigating the shipping channel in the midst of the storm, the freighter *Summit Venture* was tossed about as if it were a toy. With visibility at almost zero, Captain John Lerro quickly lost control of his vessel, and at 7:38am the ship slammed into the #2 pier of the Sunshine Skyway Bridge that spanned Tampa Bay. The violent collision knocked out more than a quarter mile of the southbound span. A huge section of the historic bridge was left dangling cantilever into the bay. Traffic on the bridge, speeding forward in spite of the intense fog, had no way of knowing the bridge was out. A Greyhound bus with a driver and 19 passengers aboard was the first vehicle over the edge, plunging 150 feet into the churning waters of Tampa Bay. Others followed in quick succession, sailing into midair and falling to the sea. Finally, one driver saw the danger and stopped his car a mere 14 inches from certain death. Another driver, whose identity has never been made known, abandoned his car and ran back toward the oncoming traffic, flailing his arms in a desperate warning to others. His actions saved untold lives.

Thirty-five people lost their lives that morning, their last moments spent in the terror of a free fall into the sea. Some died from the blunt trauma of hitting the water; others drowned, knocked unconscious before they perished. Only one person survived, purely because his pickup truck landed on the deck of the *Summit Venture.* Though badly injured, he eventually recovered.

I have often thought about the last vehicles to pass safely across that bridge before the moment of disaster. Did they think that God had spared them or that they were just lucky or that "fate" had allowed them to make it to the other side? Imagine the stories they told in the days following, and perhaps still tell to this day. And then picture those 35 people—men, women, children, teenagers—from various walks of life, some very young, some as old as 92. What did they think as their lives passed before them in a flash? Did they know Christ as Savior? Were they heaven-bound or destined for eternity without God?

When I think of that disastrous day I recall that the very night before, the evening of May 8, 1980, my own father had driven a bus across that bridge—a bus filled with over 40 passengers, all of them unaware that it would be the last night any vehicles would ever cross that span.

And what about those who stopped just in time? How many of them saw the anonymous man risking his life to warn anyone and everyone he could? In my mind he is a remarkable example of what a witness is and what a witness does.

> **What about those who stopped just in time? How many of them saw the anonymous man risking his life to warn anyone and everyone he could?**

A witness begins with a need. For the Christian witness, it is the need people have for a Savior. They are separated from God, and they need a bridge to get back into relationship with him. Not the God of a particular religion, but the one and only, true and living God who gave us his Word, the Bible, and gave us his Son, Jesus. This one true God is all-knowing, all-sufficient, all-powerful; and he has one amazing purpose toward us: to reconcile mankind to himself. For that reason he became a human being, the God/Man Jesus Christ, who lived a perfect life, died a sacrificial death and rose from the dead to open that bridge to the Father. He paid the price for our sins. For mine, for yours, for the sins of the 6.6 billion people on Planet Earth today and all the billions who preceded us. To each of us he offers the free gift of salvation, not because of any merit on our part, but simply because of his limitless grace.

Who will tell the news of this amazing grace? Remarkably, God has chosen us who have trusted in him to be his witnesses. We are the appointed givers of truth to our fellow human beings. He has determined to use us as the carriers of his message, to share our own testimonies of his saving power. We have the joy of telling others that he has made a way, and to warn those without him that the bridge is out and disaster awaits if they don't stop and turn to him. What a great responsibility! What an astonishing privilege!

Remarkably, God has chosen us who have trusted in him to be his witnesses.

Reflecting on our call to be witnesses I cannot help but think of Billy Graham. I met him this year, and I count it one of the most memorable experiences of my life. As he approaches his 90th year of life, his body is weak and his movements are limited. He gets around with the aid of a walker, slowly and deliberately. He is contemplating his final years, caring for his wife, Ruth, and thinking about the Gospel ministry he will pass on to others. A major project, the Billy Graham Library in Charlotte, North Carolina, is now in development. Visitors to the library will "walk through" the Billy Graham story—from his birth in rural North Carolina to his first days in evangelism and through his extraordinary outreach to millions of people worldwide. I accompanied Franklin Graham as he presented a "virtual tour" of the library's exhibits to his famous father. At the end of the presentation, Billy Graham said in a worn voice, "Franklin, I think it's too much about me. It needs to be more about God." I wept. I

For him, it is always about the witness—the testimony of who God is and how he offers us his very life.

thought, Billy Graham has preached the Gospel face-to-face to more people than anyone in history. He is considered by many the greatest Christian leader of the past century. And in that moment I saw why as I heard him humbly say, "It's too much about me." For him, it is always about the witness, always about the testimony of who God is and how he offers us his very life.

It's just amazing that God takes the simplest of us—from the fisherman of Galilee to a young girl from the tiny hamlet of Leslie, South Carolina—my mother. Peggy June Shillinglaw was an unusual girl from the beginning. Tender, kind and compassionate, hers was a rich heritage of many generations of Christians. Mom was a living expression of the South—its traditions, its graces. She was a soft spoken lady, but inwardly tough and resourceful, with the ability to take a soup bone and make an entire meal out of it. She was accomplished for her generation, a graduate of Winthrop College in Rock Hill, S.C. After getting her degree she went to visit her aunt and uncle in Augusta, Georgia in the summer of 1953. It was there that she met a young serviceman named Robert Nowery.

My dad is a man's man. A proud Yankee, he hails from generations of coal miners and steel mill workers. His hometown in West Virginia was the kind of place where, day after day, men went down into the mines in the darkness and came out in the darkness. Dad's generation had weathered the Great Depression, endured the food lines, struggled through discouragement and loss. My dad didn't know his own dad very well. Not because he wasn't a good man; he was there, but he was detached and distant. Dad was a gifted athlete, a football player, All-Ohio Valley Conference in high school, recipient of dozens of college offers. He settled on Mississippi State because they offered him a 6-year scholarship and as he puts it, "I knew it would take me every bit that long to graduate!" In his second year at MSU he was injured in a game and lost his scholarship. He had nowhere to go, his dream was crushed; so he signed up for the war in Korea. I've often thought that my dad was made for war. He was strong and intimidating, the sort of man you could imagine on the frontlines of battle. He was tough, focused, purposeful and boy could he fight! Like many men of his generation, Dad doesn't like to talk about Korea, didn't like watching the coverage of the Vietnam War, didn't understand the student protests that plagued America during those years. After completing his tour of duty in Korea, he was assigned to Kinley Air Force Base in Bermuda, a world away from the conflict in Asia. Little did he know his life was about to be changed forever.

He had nowhere to go, his dream was crushed; so he signed up for the war in Korea.

En route to Bermuda, Dad was sent first to Camp Gordon just outside Augusta, Georgia. There he was with his best friend Ray Dickelman on a Saturday afternoon in mid-August. As Dad says, it was "Georgia hot." Like so many service-men during that era, he stayed outside when it was hot because there was no air conditioning back then. The day before, my mom had received a call from the church she attended while visiting her aunt and uncle. Would she be willing to meet the servicemen passing through Camp Gordon and witness to them about her faith in Christ? Just pass out some coffee and sandwiches and share your testimony, the pastor suggested. I smile to think of my mom, a sweet, innocent southern girl, witnessing to battle-hardened soldiers on a military base! But she did it, and I'm certainly glad she did.

My dad still loves to tell the story of how he met my mom on that hot day in August over a half century ago. She came through, offering sandwiches and coffee, and asked if she could tell him about her faith in Christ. Ever the gentleman, he listened to her and says that he fell in love the moment he first saw her. They wrote to one another over the next year, and without having one formal date, Dad asked her to marry him. She accepted (an action that her side of the family doesn't understand to this day), and they began their life journey together. When they were still a newlywed couple my dad finally gave his heart to Christ. The love and persistent witness of a godly woman had led him to the Savior.

I smile to think of my mom, a sweet, innocent southern girl, witnessing to battle-hardened soldiers on a military base!

That's what being a witness is about. It demands the making of a decision to love someone else to the point that you tell them that on the road they're travelling the bridge is out. But there's another road, a road that leads over a bridge that can never give out, never fail. A faithful witness realizes that people die, and when they die they will either be with the Lord forever or separated from him forever. There's no middle existence. Apart from believing and receiving Christ's offer of life and salvation, there is no other way. "For there is salvation in no other,"[1] Simon Peter preached on the first Day of Pentecost.

It concerns me that I don't very often hear the clear, cogent communication of the Gospel. On several occasions at speaking engagements I have been asked to not be so "dogmatic" or "black and white" about what it means to come to Christ. One pastor even asked me to not pray at the end of my message because the strategic placement for prayer was at the beginning of the service!

A faithful witness realizes that people die, and when they die they will either be with the Lord forever or separated from him forever. There's no middle existence.

I told him, I can't do that. It causes me to wonder, why are so many churches becoming so wishy-washy about declaring the Gospel of Christ? Could it be that they don't really understand the Gospel with clarity and certainty? Are they inordinately concerned about offending people and driving them away? I have to ask, what would they be driven away from? After 30 years of ministry I am more convinced than ever that there is a great gulf fixed between us and a holy God, and that apart from Christ there is no way across that chasm. Christ's cross is the bridge. He is the Way. He is the Truth. He is the Life. He has rescued my life. I owe everything to him. And, most amazing of all, he asks me—just as he asks you—to be his witness.

Imagine Jesus asking for your help. Think of the story of the disciples when they went looking for food to satisfy the multitude. They stumble upon a little boy with a basket of fish and bread, probably packed by his mother, and they say to him, "Jesus needs your help." There were thousands upon thousands of people there that day, and the little boy could have felt so insignificant. What could he possibly do? But Jesus was asking for his help, asking him to give what he could.

The little boy could have felt so insignificant. What could he possibly do? But Jesus was asking for his help, asking him to give what he could.

He did, of course, and Jesus transformed his tiny lunch into a meal that we call the Feeding of the 5000. Is it really that different for you and me? We wonder, does he really need my help, my involvement? Does my witness really matter? If it were dependent upon us and our own ingenuity, no it wouldn't. But the strength is in him, not in us. And the power is in the Gospel itself—"the power of God unto salvation."[2]

In the summer of 2005 my mom died after suffering with Parkinson's disease for 30 years. She fell and fractured her arm and was hospitalized, and while in the hospital she contracted a staph infection. It was brutally severe and the doctors told us she had just a few days to live. In their last conversation before her homegoing, Dad said, "Peggy, what will I do without you?" In her inimitable way she smiled at him and replied, "Oh, Bob, it's OK. It's time to let me go. God put me on earth for one thing...to help you know him!" To the very end she understood the priority of sharing the Gospel, and she was a revolutionary witness.

Lesson 1:
Seize the God-given opportunities
to give away your faith.

One of the most compelling examples of revolutionary witness is the encounter between Jesus and a young Samaritan woman. The account of their conversation in John chapter 4 is loaded with lessons for every Christ follower who is serious about being effective in evangelism. Their meeting didn't last long, but in one brief interchange Jesus presented the Gospel with absolute clarity and a woman's life was forever transformed.

> *4Now he had to go through Samaria. 5So he came to a town in Samaria called Sychar, near the plot of ground Jacob had given to his son Joseph. 6Jacob's*

*well was there, and Jesus, tired as he
was from the journey, sat down by the
well. It was about the sixth hour. [7]When a
Samaritan woman came to draw water,
Jesus said to her, "Will you give me a
drink?" [8](His disciples had gone into the
town to buy food.) [9]The Samaritan
woman said to him, "You are a Jew and I
am a Samaritan woman. How can you
ask me for a drink?" (For Jews do not
associate with Samaritans.)*

When I begin a new day I try to always pray, "Lord,
let me see people the way you see them. Grant me
the wisdom to speak words of hope and life as you
did. Let me witness not simply to fulfill a responsibility
but to express my love for you. Help me to sense the
urgency of telling others how their lives can be radically, permanently changed through knowing you."

I am astonished to see so many Christians who
seem so comfortable on either end of a spectrum of
behavior. One group is at ease around non-believers,
never appropriating any opportunity to share the
Gospel with them. And, at the other end of the spectrum are the Christians who seem proud that they no
longer associate with non-Christians! Both groups are
unbalanced. To be a witness for Christ, one must get
to know people who have yet to trust in him. But when

you spend time with non-believers you must seize the moments to share God's love and truth with them. Remember, Jesus spent time with irreligious people— "publicans and sinners".[3] Of course, the "religious" crowd got upset with him for hanging out with the heathen, but Jesus gave them a categorical answer: "It is not the healthy who need a doctor, but the sick. For I have not come to call the righteous, but sinners."[4]

Today as in Jesus' day, there are common gathering places. In Jesus' day it was the community well. Recently in Africa I was reminded of what that must have been like as I watched Sudanese women walk to the wells to draw water to carry back home. I noticed that when they arrive at the well they sit on the ground or under the shade of nearby trees. It is there that they talk with friends and neighbors and catch up on the latest news. Jesus walked up to such a site 2,000 years ago and there met the Samaritan woman. In doing so, he crossed several cultural barriers. There was a barrier between men and women, much as still exists in the Arab world today. There was also a religious barrier. Jews and Samaritans had nothing to do with each other, and actually hated one another and didn't even try to hide their enmity. And worst of all in the eyes of the religious

When you spend time with non-believers you must seize the moments to share God's love and truth with them.

world, Jesus was a rabbi and the woman with whom he conversed was a prostitute. Jesus wasn't repulsed by the woman, and talking with her didn't make him non-religious. He didn't see the woman at the well as one more duty to check off of some list. He had compassion on her and seized the opportunity to give her the water of life.

Lesson 2:
Ignite interest in spiritual matters.

[10]Jesus answered her, "If you knew the gift of God and who it is that asks you for a drink, you would have asked him and he would have given you living water." [11]"Sir," the woman said, "you have nothing to draw with and the well is deep. Where can you get this living water? [12]Are you greater than our father Jacob, who gave us the well and drank from it himself, as did also his sons and his flocks and herds?" [13]Jesus answered, "Everyone who drinks this water will be thirsty again, [14]but whoever drinks the water I give him will never thirst. Indeed, the water I give him will become in him a spring of water welling up to eternal life." [15]The woman said to him, "Sir, give me this water so that I won't get thirsty and

have to keep coming here to draw water."

Jesus ignited the woman's interest with a powerful little phrase: "If you knew..." Those words unleashed her imagination, undoubtedly making her wonder what in the world he was talking about. Jesus the Son of God knew that without the water of life she had no hope, but if she received the gift her life would be totally redefined. Her thoughts were probably confused. *Living water? Never thirst again? What could this mean?* Like the women in third world countries today, she was tired of carrying that water day after day. "Sir, give me this water..." she said. She was needing help with a difficult task, and she lived a life that others at the well probably

Jesus ignited the woman's interest with a powerful little phrase: "If you knew..."

knew. Perhaps she was reminded every day that she wasn't good enough, that she didn't measure up. She was about to learn a revolutionary truth. Someone was to care about her so much and have so much compassion and mercy that he would offer himself as the source of spiritual water. It was his life. He was the water.

On a recent cross-country flight I sat next to a man who was returning to the U.S. from his second home in Latin America. I had been upgraded to first class and was settled into my seat when he walked into the cabin and sat down in the only seat left, right next to me. He was in his 70s, unkempt and eccentric, with a manner that would be off-putting to many people. It was already late, approaching midnight, but he was wired for conversation and I knew God had caused our paths to cross. He told me how his family had migrated to California back in the mid-1800s, some of the original '49ers who arrived in the days of the great Gold Rush. We talked about that history and followed several rabbit trails of interest. I learned that he was born the same year as my dad and that he, too, had fought in the Korean War. I asked about his family and the tone became more serious, almost somber. His wife had passed away from cancer, his son had overdosed on drugs.

I learned that he is a very rich man. Monetarily rich. But spiritually he is bankrupt.

Our conversation progressed further and I learned that he is a very rich man. Monetarily rich. But spiritually he is bankrupt. He finally asked that magical question, the one I sometimes hear several times a day: "What do you do?" I answered with a line I have used for decades. "I help people." He looked up at me this time. Until that moment he had talked on and on, staring at the bulkhead the entire time, occasionally pushing up the glasses that would slide down the bridge of his nose. "How's that?" he said. I said, "I help pastors and churches to meet some of their biggest challenges. I write books, I communicate to groups, I lead a leadership organization, but mostly I just help people." I could tell he was curious. He asked, "How do you do that?" In reply, I said, "First I earn their trust by proving myself trustworthy." Then I asked him, "Who do you trust?" He thought for a moment and said, "I trust only one other person on this earth other than myself, and that's my accountant." He began to pour out his sorrows and I listened intently. The loss of his wife came up again. Then as he was winding down, he said, "I have a daughter, too. I don't know where she is and don't give a damn either. All she has ever done is take from me." It broke my heart to hear that. I could tell he didn't really mean it, that he was trying to put a tough exterior on something very tender inside.

I was tired after a very long day, but it was clear that he needed to talk some more, so we did. He was so lonely, and his words were laced with regrets. He coughed constantly, so I asked about his health. "No matter," he said gruffly. I replied, "You remind me of my dad. Yes, it *does* matter. Are you sick?" He answered warily, "Yeah, I just found out I have lung cancer. I'm coming home because of that." For the remainder of that three-hour flight I did my best to show him that I truly cared. I urged him to find his daughter. "No matter what," I said, "no matter what has happened in the past, find her and end your days in contact with her."

For a few moments we were silent. Then he turned and looked at me and said, "Who are you?" I looked squarely in his eyes because I believed I was with a man just before he was to enter eternity. His bridge was out and he didn't even know it. I asked God to help me not mess this up and said, "I am Kirk Nowery." I put out my hand to shake his and as we shook hands I said, "Mr. Smith (not his real name), I was supposed to sit over there tonight. I gave up my seat to allow those people to sit together, and that put me over here. There was a reason that happened. Now please listen to me for a minute. This might be the most important conversation of your life. God loves you, he has already paid the price for your sins and you can have eternal life in heaven, in God's presence, if you will come through the cross and give your heart to him through his Son, the Lord Jesus Christ." For the remaining minutes of that flight he pondered those words. We soon landed. I gave him my card and asked him to call me if he prayed that sinner's prayer. My heart still aches for him as I write this book. The issue is vital and it is urgent, and when the bridge is out we must find a way to talk about the thing that matters most.

I believed I was with a man just before he was to enter eternity. His bridge was out and he didn't even know it.

Lesson 3:
Be a friend, not a judge.

[16]He told her, "Go, call your husband and come back." [17]"I have no husband," she replied. Jesus said to her, "You are right when you say you have no husband. [18]The fact is, you have had five husbands, and the man you now have is not your husband. What you have just said is quite true."

As God in the flesh, Jesus had every prerogative to condemn the woman for her sinful lifestyle. But he didn't. Even when he revealed specific knowledge of her, it wasn't to expose her problem but to draw her to the solution. Jesus didn't need to condemn her; the woman's own heart would do that, and she quickly tried to change the subject.

Jesus didn't need to condemn her; the woman's own heart would do that.

Lesson 4:
Stick to what's important.

[19]"Sir," the woman said, "I can see that you are a prophet. [20]Our fathers worshiped on this mountain, but you Jews claim that the place where we must wor-

ship is in Jerusalem." [21]Jesus declared, "Believe me, woman, a time is coming when you will worship the Father neither on this mountain nor in Jerusalem. [22]You Samaritans worship what you do not know; we worship what we do know, for salvation is from the Jews. [23]Yet a time is coming and has now come when the true worshippers will worship the Father in spirit and truth, for they are the kind of worshippers the Father seeks. [24]God is spirit, and his worshippers must worship in spirit and in truth." [25]The woman said, "I know that Messiah" (called Christ) "is coming. When he comes, he will explain everything to us."

The woman didn't reply directly to what Jesus said. Instead, she attempted to side-track the conversation with observations about the differences between Samaritans and Jews. But Jesus was not about to be diverted, so he turned her statements into a radical declaration about true worshippers of God. That led her to blurt out, "I know that Messiah is coming. When he comes, he will explain everything to us." Jews and Samaritans alike were anticipating Messiah's arrival. That was something they had in common; and the expectation was that Messiah would straighten out all the differences and give them all the answers. Then Jesus dropped the bombshell statement on her...

> [26]*Then Jesus declared, "I who speak to you am he."*

Lesson 5:
Present Christ openly and directly.

Imagine how the woman's heart leaped when he said those words! Imagine her thoughts, her emotions, and the realization: *I am face to face with the Son of God! Face to face with the Messiah himself.* He had communicated to her with sensitivity, yet he was direct. The challenge was to believe him and follow him. Imagine it! A rabbi asking an adulterous woman to become a "follower" of God. Surely she thought,

When she looked at Jesus' face, she knew in her heart of hearts, this is the one! This is the promised Messiah!

what kind of love is this? She was, after all, a woman who likely thought, *No one has ever really cared about me for something other than my body, about what they could take from me.* I have to believe that Satan was fighting for her simultaneously, battling with her thoughts as he fights for our thoughts every day. But when she looked at Jesus' face, she knew in her heart of hearts, this is the one! This is the promised Messiah! She believed and she was changed forever. Her passion and vision came flowing from her cleansed soul like the torrent of a waterfall. It not only changed her forever, it was a witness that changed a city. She had tasted the water of life and would never thirst again.

To be a revolutionary witness it takes a revolutionary power, and that power is in the Gospel itself. Paul wrote that "the Gospel is the power of God unto salvation."[5] The English word *power* is derived from the Greek term *dunamis*. It means something with explosive energy. It is the same root for the word *dynamite*. And spiritually speaking, that's what the Gospel is— the explosive power of God to change lives.

The Gospel is not a clever scheme or system. It is a message about a person—the central person in all of history. It is the truth that God at an appointed time had compassion on us, loved us and sent the only one who could span the broken bridge. He sent his Son, the Lord Jesus Christ, who suffered and died that we might have eternal life through him. We are his witnesses, and the Good News we bear is absolutely, positively revolutionary.

6

Revolutionary Compassion

Caring Enough to Act

Compassion is a compelling word. It comes from two Latin words that literally mean "to suffer with." To have compassion is to suffer with another person, to feel what they feel, to identify with their plight. I like the way that *Webster's* defines compassion: "Sorrow for the sufferings or troubles of another or others, accompanied by an urge to help." The last phrase is especially significant: *accompanied by an urge to help*. The truly compassionate person is motivated to act, to respond with genuine help. Compassion is not merely feeling pity for someone in need, it is doing something to intercede on that person's behalf and meet that need.

Compassion is not merely feeling pity for someone in need, it is doing something to intercede on that person's behalf and meet that need.

Jesus was the epitome of compassion, constantly connecting with the sufferings of people from all stations of life. When he looked out across the city of Jerusalem, he wept, knowing its people were like sheep without a shepherd. Throughout his earthly ministry he reached out with perfect compassion to rescue the lost, heal the sick, feed the hungry and touch the untouchables. Prompted by a heart of infinite love, he always cared enough to act.

To follow Christ is to live a life of true compassion—a life that is fueled by the desire to share his love in every way possible. It means denying yourself and taking up the cross. It means communicating encouragement to people who are down and discouraged. It means caring enough to act for the sake of the lost, the poor, the hurting and the helpless people who cross the path of your life.

Compassion for the Lost

I was about to take my first trip to the Rocky Mountains of Colorado. Growing up in South Florida, the most Dad and Mom could ever afford for a family vacation was a few days in the Florida Keys. It was there I learned my love for the sea, the crystal clear waters, the spectacular reefs; but I remember wanting so much to see the Rockies. I longed to hike in the mountains, see life in the wild, breathe in the pure, rarified air. Years later, as a young married man, I still had the desire but like my parents, I had no money. *One of these days*, I told myself. *One of these days I'm going to make it to the mountains*. Fortunately, that day came sooner than expected. Some of my buddies (guys who had both the desire and the money) told me they were going elk hunting in Colorado and they wanted me to join them. Knowing that I was next to broke but that I knew my way around a kitchen, they invited me to come along as the camp cook. I was inexpressibly excited and I immediately started to get ready to meet the challenge. I began a fitness program to get in shape for mountain climbing, I read books on hunting, and I got all my menus ready.

I must have been the laughingstock of my South Florida neighborhood–jogging down the block, dressed in heavy clothes, weighted down with my backpack and boots!

Thinking back on those days I must have been the laughingstock of my South Florida neighborhood—jogging down the block, dressed in heavy clothes, weighted down with my backpack and boots! The more I prepared, the less prepared I felt. All the reading, training and research reinforced my suspicions that it would be no easy task. But I kept up the regimen. By the day we departed I had the gear ready, the rifle sighted, and all the meal plans organized.

After a full day of travel we arrived at a ranch high

in the mountains on the western slope of the Rockies, right on the Continental Divide. I had not a clue that my life was about to intersect with a family of true-grit Coloradans, the Nicholls. Dave Nicholl was a legitimate mountain man—tall, rugged and wizened. He was coarse of manner, coarse of speech, and I had no doubt that he could talk a wild animal into submission! He was one intimidating man. Dave and his wife, Dee, had two teenage sons, Matt and Spencer. In my first day around them I sensed that other than Dee, this family didn't know God. They were lost. And as had happened so many other times in my life, my heart connected to them, compelled to find the right moment to talk to them about Christ and eternity.

As the camp cook I had a long list of responsibilities but I still got to go along on the hunting expeditions. We spent the first two days "glassing" a vast area that was the most spectacular place I had ever seen, brilliant with aspens that were already starting to turn. We strained our eyes for hours peering through powerful binoculars, captivated by the beauty but failing to spot a single elk. Coming from sea level we were still getting acclimated to the 8,000-foot altitude. We sat around the campfire, told stories, ribbed and ridiculed one another and carried on like we were kids again.

The first morning of the hunt arrived and after

breakfast at 3:30am we loaded up and headed out, making our way up barely passable logging trails. The entire group was already up on the divide for a couple of hours but Matt, one of the Nicholls' two teenage sons had compassion for me and took me to his secret hunting spot! In less than an hour my hunting was over when I harvested a bull elk. Matt helped me load it onto a truck and haul it back down to the barn. That evening the guys couldn't believe it when they saw my elk. It was beginner's luck, of course, but I wouldn't admit it to them!

The next day I realized why I was there on that mountain. It wasn't to hunt an elk but to fish for men. In those first couple of days God had prompted me to build a relationship with the Nicholl family, to have compassion for them like loving people once had compassion for my family. That morning, after everyone had headed out, Spencer Nicholl and I ate a big breakfast in the kitchen. He had been assigned to take me hiking, and I was very appreciative. We finished, cleaned up, and he asked if I was ready to go. Absolutely, I said, and we packed a lunch and were out the door within minutes. A hike, I soon learned, meant a full-day trip to a nearby summit. My lungs strained to fill with air, and my muscles ached in new places. At the top of the

The next day I realized why I was there on that mountain. It wasn't to hunt an elk but to fish for men.

mountain we sat down to have our lunch and I asked Spencer about his relationship with God. For a long time I shared my life story, my commitment to Christ and the importance of a relationship with him. Spencer had been thinking about spiritual things and God had made him ready for our conversation. We prayed, we shed some tears, and that afternoon we hiked back down the mountain long after dark. When we walked into the ranch house it was obvious that Spencer had been crying and he did his best to tell his dad about our talk about Christ. Dave Nicholl looked at his son, then turned to me and said, "Preacher, you leave my sons alone." I felt that I had shown Christ-like compassion to Spencer, but Dave had no compassion for me! There was tension between us for the rest of the week, but something was beginning to happen in Dave Nicholl's heart.

A few years later Dave called me and my friend Don Murphy and asked us to come see him. He wanted to talk to us about something important. We were eager to go back to Colorado, of course, but even more eager to hear what Dave had to say. The three of us met and there on the same mountain range where I had seen Spencer's life take a dramatic turn, Dave Nicholl told us that he, too, had committed his life to Christ. And prior to Dave's conversion, Matt Nicholl had trusted in Christ. The entire Nicholl family had been spiritually transformed! Dee Nicholl's prayers had been answered. Her husband and sons had been radically changed by the power of Christ.

Spencer's journey has been remarkable. He was recruited by Bill Bright to be the first person to carry the *Jesus* Film into Mongolia. He became the point person in a vital mission to that difficult land. He contracted a parasite and became so ill that he nearly died. But Spencer never quit. After Mongolia he went as a missionary to some of the remotest regions of Siberia! The same Good News I shared with him on that mountaintop in Colorado he has shared with thousands of others in places most of us will only read about.

The same Good News I shared with him on that mountaintop in Colorado he has shared with thousands of others in places most of us will only read about.

The Nicholl family today is totally sold out to Jesus Christ. All of the coarseness of the old Dave Nicholl is completely gone. Dave and Dee lead a weekly Bible study at the old ranch, the Big Horn. Matt and his wife are leaders in their church in Gunnison; and along with Spencer and his wife they now run the ranch as a ministry outreach and retreat for pastors and missionaries. All of them have a passion for Christ and a compassion for the lost, never forgetting that one day some years ago they too needed to be found. They, too, needed someone to point the way to Christ.

Telling someone about Christ isn't hard. Your personal testimony is your story and you don't need to complicate it with evangelistic formulas. To simply share what has happened in your life is the most meaningful and powerful thing you will ever do for someone who has yet to find life's purpose. I encourage you: be always thinking, always looking, always hoping to be a "fisher of men." You never know what will happen. I had no way of knowing what God had in store when I shared Christ with Spencer that day, and only eternity will reveal the extent of the spiritual harvest that has been reaped.

Compassion for the Poor

Let me ask you an interesting question: Would you like to get God's attention? No, it isn't a trick question. In fact, I pose the question because of a significant story in Acts chapter 10, a story about the spread of the Gospel message to the entire human race. In the city of Caesarea lived a man named Cornelius, a centurion of the Roman army. The Bible says, "He [Cornelius] and all his family were devout and God-fearing; he gave generously to those in need and prayed to God regularly."[1] One day at about three in the afternoon he had a vision. The story continues: "He distinctly saw an angel of God, who came to him and said, 'Cornelius!' Cornelius stared at him in fear. 'What is it, Lord?' he asked. The angel answered, 'Your prayers and gifts to the poor have come up as a memorial offering before God.'"² The angel then ordered Cornelius to send men to the city of Joppa to bring back Simon Peter. When the angel had left, Cornelius called three men to his house and sent them on a mission to Joppa.

What was it about Cornelius that got God's attention? It was his prayers and gifts to the poor. Cornelius, a powerful man, a commander of armed forces, had a compassionate heart and God rewarded him with the opportunity to be the first Gentile to hear the Good News of Jesus Christ. His generous gifts were a help to the poor, but an offering to God. The Bible leaves no doubt that we must pay attention to the poor, giving generously to them and looking upon them with the realization that we could just as easily be in their shoes. When we are generous with all that we have, God blesses all that we do. The Book of Deuteronomy says, "Give generously to him [a poor man among you] and do so without a grudging heart; then because of this the Lord your God will bless you in all your work and in everything you put your hand to."³

What was it about Cornelius that got God's attention? It was his prayers and gifts to the poor.

Ours is a very rich nation, but we still have the poor among us, Millions of them, in fact, and we must never forget them. They need food, clothing, shelter, employment and money. But, above all, they need the compassionate expression of Christ's love and grace. For the majority of Christians in North America, it is easy to ignore the poor. We get settled into our lives and manage to avoid them. Bill Hybels, founding pastor of Willow Creek Community Church in the outskirts of Chicago, did a survey of the congregation and discovered that fewer than 3% of adults in the church family were doing anything at all to communicate compassion to the poor. He was astounded, and he challenged the church to get out of their comfort zone and reach out to needy, disadvantaged people wherever they could find them. In one year's time, that 3% had grown to nearly 70% as two-thirds of the Willow Creek family began to practice revolutionary compassion toward the poor of greater Chicago. The impact, as you can imagine, has been phenomenal. Lives have been energized on both sides of the equation, and God has been glorified.

Can the same thing happen in your life and in your church? Yes it can. Make it so!

Compassion for the Hurting

In the early days of my ministry as a pastor I went every week (sometimes every day) to visit in the local hospitals. Strange as it may seem, I enjoyed those visits, probably because people seemed to be encouraged by even the slightest expression of concern. One day as I was leaving the county hospital in Miami, a huge complex that is one of the nation's largest medical centers, I saw a man standing in the doorway of a small ward. Our eyes met and I nodded at him, almost by reflex. As I passed by, he said, "You can't look at me, can you?" His words stopped me dead in my tracks. I turned around and as I did he stuck out his hand to shake mine. I reached out in response and he pulled me into the ward with all the strength he could muster.

I looked around the dimly-lit room and shuddered inwardly at the sight of nine men, each one covered with sores. Emaciated, their faces drawn

As I passed by, he said, "You can't look at me, can you?" His words stopped me dead in my tracks.

and gaunt, they reminded me of photos I had seen of Holocaust victims. But these men were in hospital gowns, not prison uniforms. A couple of men were seated; all the others were in their beds, staring at me as if I had just arrived from another planet. I turned to the man I had just met and asked, "Do you all have the same disease?" He replied, "Yes, but they don't know exactly what it is. It's some kind of virus. These are my friends and we're all in this together."

"I'm a minister," I announced, "can I pray with each of you?" One man replied, "Sure, but we need more than prayer. We need you to really care." I went around the room and talked with each man, doing my best to show the love and compassion of Christ. I put my hand on each man's head and said a prayer for each one. I did my best to show that I did care; and on subsequent visits to that hospital I stopped by to check on their progress. In just a few months all of them had died, but they were replaced by others with the same mystery "virus."

About a year later the AIDS crisis captured headlines and I realized what had claimed the lives of those men. There was so much misinformation and hysteria accompanying the first reports, I wondered if I had been exposed to the HIV virus during my visits. In my uncertainty I asked myself, *Did I do the right thing?* But God calmed my heart and reminded me that I had done exactly what Jesus would do—I reached out to show compassion to people who were hurting and in desperate need. I had expressed generosity in a way that only God can measure, not in dollars and cents, but in moments of "suffering with" fellow human beings.

There are hurting people in your world. Do you see them?

There are hurting people in your world. Do you see them? They often get passed by, and like that dying man who called out to me in a hospital corridor, they are at least thinking, *You can't even look at me, can you?* Choosing to look at them is the first step. It is so easy to pretend they aren't there, to do what the "religious" men did in the story of the Good Samaritan and go to the other side of the road. But revolutionary compassion in your heart keeps you from crossing that road. It keeps you on the side of the hurting people whom you can help with encouragement and care. They need to see in you the same thing the injured man saw in the Samaritan—someone, who didn't have to act but did anyway.

Look for hurting people and determine to salve their wounds in whatever way you can. The hurt may just as likely be emotional as physical. Be the one who says willingly and openly, I care about you.

Compassion for the Helpless

It's unlikely you will ever meet Joseph and Sundri, but if you could you would probably never guess where they started out on life's journey. Today, they are an attractive young couple with two lovely children. Joseph is a pastor in a major city and Sundri is a stay-at-home mom. They live in New Delhi, a teeming metropolis of 15 million, the capital of India. Just south of New Delhi is where Joseph and Sundri were born— in a leper colony. Joseph's parents, as well as Sundri's, are afflicted with leprosy, a debilitating disease that literally eats away the flesh. In India, lepers are outcasts from society, forced to live in government-designated slums. Joseph and Sundri grew up in one of those dreaded places. That is where they met as children.

Children have a built-in immunity to leprosy. Though contagious to adults, something in the divine design prevents the disease from affecting children's bodies; however, before their 12th birthday, the off-spring of leper parents must leave the colony to avoid the curse of becoming lepers themselves. Many of these children—the majority in fact—have no place to go, no one to care for them. They end up living on the streets, homeless and helpless, exposed to dangers greater than leprosy. That would have been the case with Joseph and Sundri, but someone rescued them. M. A. Thomas, revered by millions as "father to the orphans" of India, took them into one of his homes for orphaned and abandoned children. For the first time in their lives they had a secure place to live, healthy food to eat, a Christ-centered education, and a place where they could develop into purposeful adulthood. They went on to college, graduated with honors and married soon afterward. The world was open to them as never before, and they could have gone to any of India's bustling centers of commerce.

The children of leper parents must leave the colony to avoid the curse of becoming lepers themselves.

But the same compassion that had rescued them from oblivion was alive in their own hearts. Much to their surprise, Joseph and Sundri both wanted to go back to the place they hated most—the leper colony. Having been rescued themselves, they wanted to rescue other children and give them a chance to truly live. Today, Joseph and Sundri have ministries in two of the largest leper colonies in India, a ministry of compassionate medical care for those who suffer the ravages of leprosy, and a ministry of intervention for the sake of the children. Like their spiritual father, M. A. Thomas, they have now established their own home for orphaned and abandoned children.

The same compassion that had rescued them from oblivion was alive in their own hearts.

In every society are helpless people. They are in your community, too. Fatherless boys and girls who need a strong male influence in their lives. Elderly people whose children have all but forgotten them. Widows who lack the strength to do the simple tasks that were once handled by their husbands. Disabled of all ages who struggle with everyday activities. People who can't handle life on their own, people who need help.

Christ calls his followers to help the helpless. It is a revolutionary call, contrary to all the self-protecting mechanisms that cause us to draw away from needy people rather than reaching out to them. Our minds try to trick us into thinking that a helpless person is simply destined to be helpless and we should just leave things as they are. The disciples once asked Jesus about a man who had been born blind. "Rabbi," they said, "who sinned, this man or his parents, that he was born blind?" Jesus answered, "Neither this man nor his parents sinned, but this happened so that the work of God might be displayed in his life."[4] After speaking those profound words, Jesus reached out to touch the man and heal him of his blindness.

Helpless people aren't helpless because they are being punished or because God doesn't love them.

Helpless people aren't helpless because they are being punished or because God doesn't love them. Disease and disability are consequences of a fallen world, just as death itself is the consequence of sin's curse on mankind. We can't change those facts; but we can certainly do what Christ calls us to do. We can show compassion by helping the helpless and loving the unlovely. I encourage you: look for someone today who is longing for just one person to show true Christlike concern. Reach out to them. It can be transformational in their life, and in yours, too.

7

Revolutionary Generosity

Taking Hold of the Life That is Truly Life

Her name was Alexandra Scott, but everybody called her Alex. She was the founder of a charitable organization that has raised millions of dollars for pediatric cancer research. With a generous heart and a simple idea, Alex was the spark that set ablaze a movement that has touched lives in all 50 states and numerous foreign countries.

On August 1, 2004, Alex died. She was just eight years old.

Two days before her first birthday, Alex was diagnosed with neuroblastoma, a pediatric cancer that she battled for over seven years until it finally claimed her life. When she was only four years old, Alex was so grateful for the care she had received she decided to set up a lemonade stand to raise money for her local hospital in Connecticut. Alex's Lemonade Stand—and her formidable spirit—soon attracted the attention of her entire community. The lemonade stand became an annual tradition, and the idea began to spread. Hundreds of other young cancer survivors followed Alex's example and set up their own lemonade stands in cities across America. In 2005, the year after Alex died, the Alex's Lemonade Stand Foundation raised over four million dollars to find a cure for cancer. Even after she was gone, the generosity of an exceptional little girl was still yielding huge dividends.

It would have been easy for Alex to feel sorry for herself, to become withdrawn, to think that she was being punished by God. But she didn't.

Alex Scott embodied revolutionary generosity. She had a noble spirit, a kind heart and a determination to act, not merely out of desire for self-preservation but mainly to help as many other children as possible. Her example reminds us that true generosity is both a quality and a practice. It is a quality void of complaint, full of gratitude and driven by concern. And it is a practice that will not let one sit still and do nothing while others are in need.

As a Christ-follower, I am inspired by the life of young Alexandra Scott because I see Christ-like compassion in her. It would have been easy for Alex to feel sorry for herself, to become withdrawn, to think that she was being punished by God. But she didn't. Instead she was remarkably generous, giving of herself even when her body was weak and her energy level so depleted. She was open to others, willing to share and determined to give all that she could give.

In comparison with little Alex, who among us doesn't feel more blessed and more capable of demonstrating generosity? I know that I do. And let's be honest about this: relatively speaking, all of us are rich. We're rich in ways that previous generations could only dream about; and there's a purpose underlying the blessings we have received. Put it into the context of this **God makes us rich so that we can be generous**. powerful verse of Scripture: "You will be made rich in every way so that you can be generous on every occasion, and through us your generosity will result in thanksgiving to God."[1] What a revolutionary thought! *God makes us rich so that we can be generous.* Of course, the riches given to us by God are not just material or monetary riches, and the generosity we express is not just material or monetary. It is multidimensional, and its impact directs hearts to thank God, not to praise any human being.

The subtitle of this chapter is "Taking Hold of the Life That Is Truly Life." That isn't just some clever line I came up with to capture your attention. It is actually a direct quote from the Bible, part of the Apostle Paul's first letter to his son in the faith, Timothy. In the concluding verses of that memorable epistle, Paul wrote,

> *"Command those who are rich in this present world not to be arrogant nor to put their hope in wealth, which is so uncertain, but to put their hope in God, who richly provides us with everything for our enjoyment. Command them to do good, to be rich in good deeds, and to be generous and willing to share. In this way they will lay up treasure for themselves as a firm foundation for the coming age, so that they may take hold of the life that is truly life."[2]*

Notice that Paul begins with a powerful word: "Command..." He doesn't say "Suggest..." or "Propose..." or "Advise..." No, he says, "Command..." And specifically, "Command those who are rich in this present world..." In other words, tell them categorically that this is not optional; it is an absolute directive from God. The recipients of this command are identified as people "who are rich in this present world." In our day, who would that include? To underscore a point I made earlier, I think it includes a lot more people than we might realize. According to a recent report in *Money* magazine, in the U.S. today there are more than 7.5 million millionaires! Yes, you read that correctly. And in addition to all those millions of millionaires are tens of millions of people whose net worth is in the hundreds of thousands of dollars. We have pension plans, 401K plans, IRAs, investment portfolios, houses and land, yet we still fret about the future! God's word of admonition is clear: Don't be arrogant and don't put your hope in wealth because it is so uncertain. Instead, put your hope in God. He, after all, is the one who provides us with everything in the first place.

Let's get back to that important message from Paul. He continues: "Command them to do good, to be rich in good deeds, and to be generous and willing to share." Those who are materially rich in this present world are commanded to be spiritually rich as well— rich in good deeds. By showing generosity and by demonstrating a willingness to share, they earn far more of a return than dollars in a bank account or equity in a property. The pay-off is eternal: "In this way they will lay up treasure for themselves as a firm foundation for the coming age, so that they may take hold of the life that is truly life." There's the promise: treasure in the coming age, riches in heaven. And there's the added benefit: taking hold of the life that is truly life.

Those who are materially rich in this present world are commanded to be spiritually rich as well— rich in good deeds.

Taking hold of the life that truly life. What exactly does that mean? I think it means experiencing in this earthly life the profound reality of our eternal life in Christ. The life that is truly life is the life that never ends, the life that has no limitations, the life that goes infinitely beyond the boundaries of this temporal existence. One day this earthly life will end for every one of us. Whether by disease or accident or simply by our bodies giving out in old age, we all leave this existence. But, thankfully, it doesn't end here. And, as we are taught in 2 Corinthians, to be absent from the body is to be present with the Lord. We shift from one dimension into another. That other dimension, I believe, is the life that is truly life; and I think that God lets us start living it right here and now. When we receive the gift of eternal life in Christ, we don't wait to get it upon graduation from earth. We get it immediately, and we begin to live it immediately. Jesus came to give us life and give it abundantly—not physical life, but spiritual life—the life that is truly life.

When we give generously we express the character of God.

This life that is truly life has a direct link to generosity. When we give generously we express the character of God, and what others see in us is a reflection of eternity's values and heaven's treasures. It has huge implications, far greater in worth than any possession of this world. If we really, truly get our minds and hearts around that fact it can have a transformational effect. It drives me to check my motives and to think very seriously about why I should give.

My friend Bill Hybels is perhaps the most influential pastor in America. Over most of the past two decades, Willow Creek Community Church, the ministry he founded in Barrington, Illinois, has been the nation's largest congregation. With a total weekend attendance exceeding 20,000 worshippers, Willow Creek equals a mid-size U.S. city. It is a remarkable fellowship of believers, and Bill is a unique pastor. When I think of him, I think first of generosity. No other Christian leader has done more for more people. Bill has always gone out of his way to bless and benefit others, and I

Most people can be categorized as givers or takers.

think it's because he understands the true motivations underlying a generous life. Recently I heard Bill speak on the subject, "7 Reasons Why I Give." With his permission, I'm going to paraphrase his insights on this vital topic. Here's what Bill had to say...

Reason #1:
I like how I feel about myself when I give.

It may sound narcissistic, but there's no getting around the fact that it feels good to give. Whenever you give, it differentiates you from the takers; and the fact is, most people can be categorized as givers or takers. As a giver, you put yourself in alignment with God himself whose very character motivates him to give. "For God so loved the world, he gave his one and only Son."[3]

Reason #2:
The one I surrendered my life to
instructs me to be a giver.

Jesus epitomized what it means to be a giver and he taught his followers that "it is more blessed to give than to receive."[4] If I have fully committed my life to Christ, I've given him all of me, not just a part. When he says something, I need to take it seriously, I need to recognize that it isn't optional. With him, giving isn't optional, it is essential. He gives us a new set of priorities, a new perspective; and when I recognized that he wanted me to give I didn't respond kicking and screaming, feeling that it was a tax or a heavy burden. He had put in me a new heart and I felt a new way. Some people don't have that story. They came to Christ after they made a lot of money and it skewed their way of looking at giving. I remember one guy who said, "I make way too much money to make

Instead of allowing our standard of living to determine our standard of giving we must allow our standard of giving to determine our standard of living.

tithing ever happen!" I felt sorry for him because he won't ever know his full redemptive identity. Someone else said, "I just don't make enough money to tithe." I asked how much more would you need, and he said $5,000. It made me remember Jesus' words, "If you'll be faithful in the little things..."[5] We've gotten things reversed. Instead of allowing our standard of living to determine our standard of giving we must allow our standard of giving to determine our standard of living.

Reason #3:
I made a covenant with God
and with you as your pastor.

The participating membership form I filled out included a commitment to give a full 10% of my income to the church. That is meaningful, and I don't want to be included with a group called covenant breakers. Ezekiel 5 has some serious things to say about such people. You must take vows seriously whether it involves your money, your marriage or your children. Our word should be good enough; if a commitment is made, a commitment should be fulfilled.

Reason #4:
I give in order to position myself
for God's blessing and protection.

I am very mindful of the promises in Scripture

associated with giving. Read Malachi chapter 3 and you'll see it very clearly. God says, if you honor me with giving I will honor you with blessing and protection. I see so many wonderful examples of this. Often they are examples of God keeping things going. We had a Suburban that God kept going for 200,000 miles. We gave it to another couple and they drove it for another 100,000 miles. It's probably still going somewhere today. Someone will say, "Bill, that's naive." I don't think so, because I know it's how God works. For 35 years at Willow God has protected and blessed us. Why would I want to change that now? I choose to keep myself under that umbrella.

Reason #5:
I believe in the vision of our church.

The Scripture declares that you need to be faithful to your church, and I'm faithful; but I'm also motivated by a love for our vision. I grew up in a church that was jarred out of a 40-year nap in order to really wake up. Now I see thousands of people on our campus involved in counseling, teaching and all types of ministry. There's a conference here right now where 2,600 youth pastors are gathered. There are hundreds of people meeting to deal with the AIDS crisis in Africa. We have a vision to see irreligious people turned into fully devoted followers of Jesus Christ, and it's happening. Think seriously about where you are if...

— No one is coming to Christ regularly
— Christ followers aren't growing
— Volunteers aren't putting on towels to serve Christ
— The lonely aren't being enfolded
— Bold prayers aren't being prayed
— The sermons are pointless
— The poor aren't being cared for
— The whole place feels devoid of the Spirit of God

It's actually easy to be generous, and you should be generous wherever you are, but it's even better when you're in a church where the vision inspires you to generosity.

You should be generous wherever you are, but it's even better when you're in a church where the vision inspires you to generosity.

Reason #6:

I want to be an example to my children.

My mom and dad were examples in their generosity. On Sunday morning when we went to church there would always be five envelopes laid out—one for each of us. Because they gave, I learned to give, and that's what we have taught our children. It's what I want our grandchildren to learn as well.

Reason #7:

I want to one day hear God say, "Well done."

I look forward to that final commendation from the Lord. When I sort out what I'm living for, I can tell you that for me it's not for here...it's for there, for what lies ahead at the end of this journey. All I want anymore is God's commendation. Can you imagine him saying, "I gave you material resources and you dropped the ball"? I don't want that. I want to hear, "Well done." I tell you, my friend, you can make decisions now that make that day quite predictable. I have never seen anyone drift toward generosity. It comes through decision. It comes through commitment.

To everything Bill said, I simply add, Amen! It drives us to ask, How can we as believers in North America practice revolutionary generosity? Let me share several key thoughts I've discovered:

Respond to need, not to pressure.

Whenever I sort through the day's mail there is nearly always an appeal from some charitable organization asking me for money. Most are worthy causes that merit consideration, but a surprising percentage are prone to manipulating the emotions to induce a response. Some even resort to a sky-is-falling urgency, giving me the impression that if I don't write out that check *right now* the whole ministry is going to collapse. Remarkably, there are organizations that use this approach month after month; and, apparently, people keep on responding to their "urgent" appeals. At times, urgency is real and it can seem almost palpable; but that is the exception in life, not the rule. More needs come to us with an unspoken hope than a shouted demand.

The generous giver is prompted to give by seeing a need and being touched by it. There is often an emotional element, but the primary motive is spiritual in nature. Giving, after all, is never to be done out of pressure or compulsion; it is a matter of grace, not law. We are to give because we want to give, love

> **The generous giver is prompted to give by seeing a need and being touched by it.**

to give, and are grateful we can give. My children, Ashley and Matt, weren't forced into going to the Sudan. No one had to drum anything into their minds or assault them with desperate pleas. They had been praying to know the will of God, opening themselves up to the possibilities of something revolutionary, and God answered their prayers by showing them a need and calling them to meet it. So it is with every believer.

Have an open heart and an open hand.

Openness is willingness, and nothing pleases God more than a heart that willingly yields to him and a hand that willingly gives to him. If one claims to have an open heart but is not willing to have an open hand, something is wrong, for the two should be inseparable.

God doesn't force us to yield to him or give to him. He created us as free moral beings who constantly exercise the power of choice. As C. S. Lewis explained: "God has made it a rule for himself that he won't alter people's character by force. He can and will alter them—but only if the people will let him. He would rather have a world of free beings, with all its risks, than a world of people who did right like machines because they couldn't do anything else. The more we succeed in imagining what a world of perfect automatic beings would be like, the more, I think, we shall see his wisdom."

A willing yieldedness to God can make a radical impact in a church, a community, even a nation.

A willing yieldedness to God can make a radical impact in a church, a community, even a nation. That was the result when God's people gave toward the building of the temple. King David personally led the "capital campaign" because as the leader he had to set the example, and he had to make the appeal in the most memorable way possible. It was the biggest project of its kind ever undertaken—a "palatial struc-

ture not for man but for the Lord God."[6] The construction materials were amazing—gold, silver, onyx,
turquoise and precious stones. No other building on
earth would be like it, and it could only be built by people with open hearts and open hands. King David
proved his own commitment by dedicating all his
kingly wealth and his personal treasures to the project.
The other leaders, profoundly affected by his example,
began to give with the same intensity. And when the
offering had been received, the Bible tells us that "the
people rejoiced at the willing response of their leaders,
for they had given freely and wholeheartedly to the
Lord."[7] With a heart full of praise, David said, "Who am
I, and who are my people, that we should be able to
give as generously as this? Everything comes from
you, and we have given you only what comes from
your hand."[8]

King David inspired his people in many ways,
especially through his generosity, for it was something
each person could do. Few could be the kind of military commander or discerning judge that David was;
but everyone could give generously, and they were
motivated to do so by his example. When you give
willingly—with an open heart and an open hand—God
can use your example to encourage others to do the
same.

Take money seriously, but not too seriously.

I was recently passing through an airport terminal when an image on television caught my eye—thousands of dollar bills floating through the air, falling like green confetti on the busy street of a major city. "It's Raining Money" read the caption, and sure enough it was. A man had decided to express his magnanimity by throwing $10,000 in cash out the window of a tall building. The result, of course, was chaotic. The local authorities didn't appreciate his gesture of goodwill and he was fined—for littering!

Money, as we know so well, can be both a blessing and a curse. It is essential to daily life, but we are easily prone to become obsessive about it. We are wise to remember that Proverbs cautions, "Don't wear yourself out to get rich."[9] Money is important, but it isn't everything, and it can't bring true satisfaction. If you take money too seriously it can cloud your judgment, alter your motives and steal the joy that generosity brings. The spiritually-balanced believer recognizes that money is a means to an end, not the end itself.

Proverbs cautions, "Don't wear yourself out to get rich."

Perhaps you have heard it said that "money is the root of all evil." I have heard that statement countless times. But that is not what the the Bible says. The verse actually reads: "For *the love of money* is a root of all kinds of evil."[10] The problem is not with money;

the problem is with loving it. To love money is to place a value on it that exceeds what God says it is worth. If we love money we can never give with a smile, we can never be free and joyous. God's desire is not that we go through life simply collecting things and holding on to them. Instead, he wants us to give and give and give, just as he himself does.

True generosity is joyful. It is prompted by what a person "has decided in his heart to give, not reluctantly or under compulsion, for God loves a cheerful giver."[11] Once again we see that priority of wholehearted willingness—the attitude that says, "I'm giving because I want to give, I am delighted to give and I'm grateful I can give." When this attitude really takes root in us, the result truly is revolutionary.

Act out of love, not out of guilt.

> I couldn't bring myself to even go into my local Starbucks and buy a cup of coffee, knowing that one cup cost the equivalent of a day's wages in Sudan.

When I returned to the comforts of life in the U.S. after visiting my son Matt in Africa, I had a hard time dealing with some of the simplest things. For several days I couldn't bring myself to even go into my local Starbucks and buy a cup of coffee, knowing that one cup cost the equivalent of a day's wages in Sudan.

But I was responding out of unfounded guilt. God gently reminded me that Africa's poverty is not the result of America's prosperity; and his desire is that we act rationally, not react irrationally. The generous revolutionary is motivated by the love of Christ, a transcendent power far greater than the downward pull of guilt.

Love is the greatest force in all of creation. It is the power that surpasses all others in breadth, depth and height. Nothing compares to it, for it expresses the very essence of the one who spoke everything into existence: "God is love" says 1 John 4:16. Love is the

Why should we give? Above all, because of love.

reason God gave his one and only Son: "God demonstrated his own love for us in this: While we were still sinners, Christ died for us."[12] Love is the fruit of the Spirit.[13] Love is the greatest of the virtues.[14] Love is the hinge of the Scriptures. As Jesus explained, "'Love the Lord your God with all your heart and with all your soul and with all your mind.' This is the first and greatest commandment. And the second is like it: 'Love your neighbor as yourself.' All the Law and the Prophets hang on these two commandments."[15]

Considering all these truths, why should we give? Above all, because of love—a love for God, a love for his work, and a love for his kingdom to come and his will to be done.

Be a river, not a reservoir.

Believers are channels, not containers. God's love and grace are to flow through us, not be held in us. As stewards, our compelling desire must be to constantly give from the river of God's blessings coursing through our lives. We are simply passing on what God has passed to us.

Imagine how the disciples felt when Jesus took those five loaves of bread and two fish and turned them into a feast for thousands. Think of the hilarious joy they experienced in handing out food to the hungry, seeing God multiply it as long as they kept sharing. What a wonderful picture of what it's like for us when we give from the endless resources he entrusts to our care.

God wants to use you as a channel carrying his love and truth—and the more open the channel, the more blessed you will be. What matters most is that we care about what matters to God—the eternal souls of people. If they don't have him, they don't have hope. Don't forget, heaven will be populated with people. There won't be any sermons or committees or business meetings. But there will be worship services as the redeemed of all the ages give him endless praise. What an amazing picture! Until that day, we must heed Christ's call and take up the cause of revolutionary generosity.

REFERENCES

Chapter 1

1 Romans 12:1-2
2 Philippians 3:20
3 Philippians 3:12-14

Chapter 2

1 1 Corinthians 6:19-20
2 Psalm 24:1
3 Deuteronomy 8:18
4 Luke 12:15
5 Colossians 3:1
6 1 Timothy 6:7
7 Matthew 6:20
8 2 Peter 1:4
9 1 Corinthians 4:2
   (NASV)
10 Mark 12:43-44
   (NKJV)
11 1 Chronicles 29:3
12 Luke 6:38
13 Ephesians 5:15-16
14 1 Corinthians 4:2
15 Mark 10:42-45
16 Ephesians 1:1
17 Colossians 1:2
18 Daniel 6:4
19 Colossians 1:7
20 1 Corinthians 10:31

Chapter 3

1 John 10:30
2 John 14:9
3 John 14:6
4 Acts 4:12
5 1 Corinthians 15:19
6. Matthew 19:30; 23:12
7 Proverbs 11:25
8 Philippians 1:12-14

Chapter 4

1 Matthew 6:19-21
2 Mark 12:43-44
3 Matthew 22:15-16
4 Matthew 22:17
5 Matthew 22:18-19
6 Matthew 22:20
7 Matthew 22:21a
8 Matthew 22:21b
9 Matthew 22:21

Chapter 5

1 Acts 4:12
2 Romans 1:16
3 Matthew 9:11
4 Luke 5:32
5 Romans 1:16

Chapter 6

1 Acts 10:2
2 Acts 10:4
3 Deuteronomy 15:10
4 John 9:3

Chapter 7

1 2 Corinthians 9:11
2 1 Timothy 6:17-19
3 John 3:16
4 Acts 20:35
5 Luke 16:10
6 1 Chronicles 29:1
7 1 Chronicles 29:9
8 1 Chronicles 29:14
9 Proverbs 23:4
10 1 Timothy 6:10
11 2 Corinthians 9:7
12 Romans 5:8
13 Galatians 5:22
14 1 Corinthians 13:13
15 Matthew 22:40

Discovery Guide

Putting Revolutionary Truths into Practice

The purpose of the Discovery Guide is to guide you through an in-depth examination of the seven qualities presented in *Revolutionary Generosity*. The seven sections of the Discovery Guide correspond to the book's seven chapters; however, the questions and insights are based upon each chapter's theme (Commitment, for example), not upon the exact content of the chapter itself. The intention is to give you something more, something deeper. In each section you'll meet biblical characters who personify the various qualities—real-life revolutionaries who put the principles into practice. And following that you will find questions related to the revolution in your own life.

As you make your way through the Discovery Guide you will grow in wisdom and gain understanding of important truths. I encourage you to read the entire book and complete this entire guide because it will maximize the benefit you receive. May God empower you to live a revolutionary life!

Discovering Revolutionary Commitment

Paul: A Real-Life Revolutionary

The story and contributions of the apostle Paul are well known to most Christians. Because of his travels, his teachings, and his correspondence, Christendom was solidly established in the first century, much of the New Testament was written, and a foundation of biblical teaching was laid for believers then and now. His was truly a life of revolutionary commitment.

Read Paul's own words, describing the path of his life, in Acts 26:1-20.

Based on this passage, and any others you may know, what characterized Paul's life before his conversion on the way to Damascus?

_____

_____

_____

_____

How does Paul describe his response to Jesus, in Acts 26:19-20?

_____

_____

_____

_____

_____

In Acts 9, we find Luke's description of the conversion and early ministry of the newly converted Paul (still known as Saul at the time). According to Acts 9:22-30, what were the first days of his ministry like?

_____

_____

_____

Read the following verses, for a brief summary of Paul's experience in spreading the gospel:

2 Corinthians 6:4-5; 7:5; 11:23-29; 4:8-9

Why do you believe Paul could write, as he did in 2 Corinthians 4:8-9, that he was "hard pressed but not crushed; perplexed, but not in despair; persecuted, but not abandoned; struck down, but not destroyed?"

_____

_____

_____

What common theme can you see in these verses, penned by the apostle Paul?

1 Corinthians 2:2

Galatians 2:20

Philippians 1:18

Philippians 1:20-21

2 Timothy 2:8

_____

_____

Paul was equipped and empowered to accomplish great things even in the face of great difficulty because he was committed...not to a cause, not to a religious system, not to a book or program, but to Jesus Christ. Jesus was the Lord who spoke to him on the road to Damascus, drawing a line in the sand and calling Saul to a life of total commitment to him. When Saul said yes, his life became revolutionary. The commitment to Christ confirmed the course he would take.

Your Real-Life Revolution

Have you made a commitment to Jesus Christ? Was your experience at all like the Damascus road experience of Paul? Describe some of the highlights of your own "Damascus road."

Saul was traveling, on his way to persecute more believers. What were you doing before God met you?

_____

_____

_____

Saul was blinded by a light and terrified by the audible voice of God. What were the circumstances of your first "meeting" with God, what happened that brought you toward trusting in him for salvation?

_____

_____

_____

Saul's friends led him by the hand into Damascus, where a believer named Ananias explained what had happened to him and what God was calling him to. Who led you by the hand and explained the things of God to you early in your Christian life?

_____

_____

_____

Saul immediately obeyed God, and soon began preaching to others about the gospel of Jesus Christ. In what ways were you immediately obedient to God following your conversion to faith? What types of changes characterized your life following your conversions?

_____

_____

_____

_____

"The Christ-life is not lived only on the basis of a one-time commitment. It demands the discipline of constant commitment, constant surrender. There is, of course, a one-time commitment of one's life to Christ in the moment faith is first exercised. However, there's so much more...I can say that I have surrendered my life to Christ; but I can also truthfully say that I am still surrendering, day by day, moment by moment." (Revolutionary Generosity, pages 34-35)

What does this kind of daily surrender look like in your life?

_____

_____

_____

_____

What do the words of Jesus in Luke 9:23 mean in your life—practically, specifically, what does that mean, or what would you like it to mean in your daily routine?

_____

_____

_____

_____

_____

_____

_____

Read Philippians 3:7-16.

How would you summarize Paul's commitment in this passage?

_____

_____

_____

What attitudes or perspectives did Paul possess that would have strengthened and sustained his commitment?

_____
_____
_____
_____

Describe Paul's convictions about the past, the present, and the future.

Past:

_____
_____

Present:

_____
_____

Future:

_____
_____

Is God calling you to something new, something difficult, something bigger than before? What would revolutionary commitment look like in your life?

_____
_____
_____
_____
_____
_____

Reviewing what you've observed about Paul's attitudes, which ones stand out to you as worthy of adopting into your life? How would each one affect your commitment to God's work in and through you?

_____

_____

_____

_____

Read Philippians 2:12-13, and meditate on the meaning of verse 13.

Spend a few minutes in prayer, seeking God's guidance and affirming your commitment to obeying him. If you'd like, follow this pattern, outlined in Chapter 1 of the book:

- *Listen to God's instructions, exhortations, and encouragements to you*

- *Surrender, verbally and decisively, your life and efforts to him*

- *Sacrifice, giving up anything that hinders your commitment to him*

- *Commit yourself to obedience, and to faith that acts*

- *Pray, asking God for endurance and help in carrying out your commitments to him*

Discovering Revolutionary Stewardship

The Two Servants: Real-Life Revolutionaries

In Luke 19:11-27 (and in a similar parable in Matthew 25:14-30), Jesus told his listeners a story about a king who left ten servants in charge of substantial sums of money. To each one, he gave the instruction, "Put this money to work, until I come back." The parable recounts the results produced by three different servants. The first two servants generated 100% returns on the king's investment, doubling what had been entrusted to them. The third servant, fearing the king's wrath and unwilling to risk potential loss, had literally wrapped up the money he'd been given and simply returned to the king exactly the same sum. The first two servants were commended for their stewardship and rewarded for their faithfulness. The last servant, however, was rebuked for his foolishness and waste, and sent away from the king.

This important parable illustrates the value God places on stewarding properly and faithfully the resources he gives those who trust in him. We, like the servants, have been entrusted with substantial resources, and have been instructed to "Put this to work until I come back." While the parable speaks of money in order to clearly illustrate the concept of stewardship, we know from the whole counsel of God's Word that believers have been entrusted with much more than money to put to work until Christ returns. The Bible is filled with stories of men and women who managed resources and maximized opportunities to the glory of God. There are many biblical examples, but we'll focus our study today on a group of impoverished believers, seven willing servants, and an eccentric desert-dwelling preacher. From their examples we can learn much about the principles and priority of stewardship.

The Stewardship of Our Resources

To be sure, a great deal of stewardship is related to the use of our money and material possessions. The fact that Jesus spoke of money in his parable testifies both to its importance and its commonness in the issue of stewardship. Jesus spoke in those terms because everyone would understand them. We can all relate to the value, the risk, and the rewards related to money and material wealth.

Read the story of a group of Christians who were commended for their faithful stewardship of financial resources in 2 Corinthians 8:1-5.

What are three words you would use to characterize the Macedonians' attitudes about giving financially?

_____

_____

_____

The Macedonian churches included the fellowships at Philippi, Thessalonica, and Berea. For a closer look at each of these cities and the establishment of the churches there, read Acts 16 and 17.

Returning to 2 Corinthians 8:1-5, what is the basis of Paul's commendation, according to verse 5?

_____

_____

_____

_____

What does verse 4 indicate about the Macedonian believers' beliefs about giving?

"they _____ with us for the _____ of sharing in this service to the saints" (NIV)

In this second letter to the church at Corinth, Paul uses the example of the Macedonian churches to exhort the Corinthians to similar generosity and stewardship. How does 2 Corinthians 9:7 summarize a proper perspective on financial stewardship?

_____

_____

_____

_____

_____

The Stewardship of Our Spiritual Gifts

Infinitely more valuable than material wealth, the spiritual gifts believers are given by the Holy Spirit must be wisely, generously, and faithfully exercised in a believer's life. With wise stewardship and disciplined investment, these gifts, like the money in Jesus' parable, can produce an abundant return.

The Book of Acts records the early life of the first congregation of believers, the first days of the new Christian faith. It's an immensely valuable book, not just in terms of history and perspective, but because of the insight it provides into the practical working out of faith in fellowship. Acts 6 records one of the first roadblocks the early church leaders encountered, as they worked to organize and shepherd a community of Christ-followers. Read Acts 6:1-7.

What problem was encountered?

_____

_____

_____

What solution was found?

_____

_____

_____

To what did the apostles give their attention and time?

_____

_____

_____

_____

What were the responsibilities of the seven servants?

_____

_____

_____

What were the qualifications of the seven?

_____

_____

_____

What was the result of this division of responsibilities (verse 7)?

_____

_____

_____

What do you believe this passage teaches about using your spiritual gifts within the community of believers?

_____

_____

_____

_____

Read Ephesians 4:11-16. What reasons are given for exercising our spiritual gifts?

_____

_____

_____

The Stewardship of Our Words

Words are important to God. We see it in Genesis, when he spoke the universe into existence. We know it by his audible communication to his people in the Old Testament. We share with the psalmist a desire to worship God with words: "Let the words of my mouth...be acceptable in your sight." And we join the author of Hebrews, as we "offer to God a sacrifice of praise—the fruit of lips that confess his name." Words are a commodity. They can be priceless or worthless, and believers in Jesus do well to maximize every opportunity to spend them wisely.

One of the finest examples of a man who used words to their fullest potential was John the Baptist. Read about John's message and ministry in John 1:19-34.

The legacy of John the Baptist is inspiring. Each of the gospels records his ministry, and in each one we see the consistency and clarity of his message. Read Luke 3:2-14. What was John's message?

_____

_____

_____

_____

What was the response to John's preaching, seen in
Luke 3:15?

_____

_____

_____

_____

According to John 1:20, how did John respond to the
public's inquiries about him?

_____

_____

_____

_____

Read Luke 3:16-18. How is John's message summa-
rized in verse 18?

_____

_____

_____

_____

_____

_____

_____

Read John 1:29 and 1:35. What words would you use to characterize John the Baptist?

_____

_____

_____

_____

Read Colossians 4:5-6 and I Peter 3:15. What attitudes and actions are believers called to in these passages?

Attitudes

_____

_____

_____

_____

Actions

_____

_____

_____

_____

Your Real-Life Revolution

The faithful steward manages resources and maximizes opportunities. What resources and opportunities have you been given in each of these areas?

Money and Possessions:

Resources:

_____
_____
_____
_____

Opportunities:

_____
_____
_____
_____

Spiritual Gifts:

Resources:

_____
_____
_____
_____

Opportunities:

_____
_____
_____
_____

Words:

Resources:

_____
_____
_____
_____

Opportunities:

_____
_____
_____
_____

What would it mean for you to practice revolutionary stewardship...

Of your money and possessions?

_____
_____
_____
_____

Of your spiritual gifts?

_____
_____
_____
_____

Of your words?

_____

_____

_____

_____

Spend some time in prayer, thanking God for the resources and opportunities he has given you, and seeking his guidance, discernment, and wisdom in how you can manage and maximize all that he has entrusted to your stewardship.

Discovering Revolutionary Servanthood

Jesus: A Real-Life Revolutionary

Without question or doubt, Jesus Christ provides in his life, ministry, death, and resurrection the supreme example of servanthood. There is simply no comparison to the Creator of the universe leaving behind the glory of heaven to take on the human form, living in its limitations and ultimately suffering to the point of a violent and unjust death to make a way for men and women to know and relate to God.

Read Mark 10:45. What was Jesus' stated purpose here?

_____

_____

_____

Jesus Christ came to serve. He came to sacrifice, to die on the cross in order to bring forgiveness and atonement for sins. But he also came to serve. Jesus was a servant, not just in his death but in his entire life and ministry on earth. In his example we see the marks of a true servant, the fundamental qualities necessary for real servanthood.

Read John 13:1-17.

According to verse 1, what was Jesus preparing to show His disciples?

_____

_____

_____

_____

In your own words, describe what this scene would have looked like. Can you imagine being one of the disciples, or an observer (perhaps the owner of the house)? What would you have seen and smelled and heard that night?

_____

_____

_____

_____

_____

Have you ever had your feet washed, or washed another person's feet? What was that experience like? If you've never experienced it, what do you imagine it would be like?

_____

_____

_____

_____

_____

_____

What instruction does Jesus give the disciples in verses 14-15?

_____

_____

_____

_____

Washing feet is not a common courtesy or act of service in Western culture today. What are some acts of service you could do that would be comparable to the kind of service Jesus performed that day?

_____

_____

_____

_____

Read Philippians 2:5-11.

What qualities of servanthood are exemplified by Christ here?

_____

_____

_____

_____

How did Jesus humble himself?

_____

_____

_____

The prophet Isaiah provided a remarkably clear picture of the promised Messiah. Though many in Jesus' day missed the signs, it is clear that Jesus was the one spoken of hundreds of years before in the writings of Isaiah and other Old Testament prophets. Read Isaiah 53, and record the descriptions of Jesus in each of these verses:

v. 2-3

_____

_____

_____

v. 7

_____

_____

_____

v. 10

_____

_____

_____

In Isaiah we see both the humility and the obedience of Jesus the Messiah. Read Hebrews 10:5-7 and Matthew 26:39. What did Jesus experience as he exercised obedience to the Father?

_____

_____

_____

Obedience to God was not a discipline Jesus practiced only in His death; it was a mark of his entire life and ministry. Read the following verses and record what Jesus says about obeying the Father.

John 4:34

_____

_____

_____

_____

John 5:30

_____

_____

_____

_____

John 6:38

_____

_____

_____

_____

Your Real-Life Revolution

Do you think others who know you would describe you as a servant?

_____

_____

_____

Write about a recent experience when you took on the role of a servant. What were the circumstances? What did you do? What did you sacrifice? How did it feel?

_____

_____

_____

_____

Is there a relationship or an area of responsibility in which you may be called to servanthood right now?

_____

_____

_____

_____

Read 1 John 3:16-18. What would it mean in your particular situation to "love with actions and in truth?"

_____

_____

_____

_____

Read Romans 12:9-10. How would loving people as it is described here affect your serving of others?

_____

_____

_____

_____

Philippians 2:3-4 provides a good definition of humility in practice. How would you put it in your own words?

_____

_____

_____

_____

What would humility, as defined in Philippians 2:3-4, look like in your life and particularly in your opportunities for serving?

_____

_____

_____

_____

How does Jesus define love for him in John 14:15?

_____

_____

_____

_____

Read 1 John 5:2-3 and 1 John 3:23.

Recalling the earlier study, what was Jesus showing his disciples when he washed their feet?

_____

_____

_____

Does obedience play a part in your service to others? How?

_____

_____

_____

_____

We are called to a life of revolutionary servanthood. It is counter to our human nature, of course. We want to be served, not to serve. We want to receive, not to give. But Christ calls us to something higher.... The natural urge is against being a servant; but Christ in us gives us the power to overcome that urge and live like he lived. (Revolutionary Generosity, pg. 56)

Five Motivations for Revolutionary Servanthood

We serve because we're forgiven.

How have you been forgiven?

_____

_____

_____

_____

Spend a few minutes praying and/or journaling God's forgiveness of you.

Are there areas in which you need to seek God's forgiveness? Which areas?

_____

_____

_____

_____

How does God's forgiveness motivate you toward serving others?

_____

_____

_____

_____

We serve because we're blessed.

How have you been blessed?

_____

_____

_____

_____

Spend a few minutes praying and/or journaling about God's blessings in your life.

What are some ways in which God's blessings motivate you toward serving others?

_____

_____

_____

_____

How can you use God's blessings to serve others?

_____

_____

_____

_____

We serve because we're free.

What does your spiritual freedom mean to you?

_____

_____

_____

_____

From what has Christ set you free?

_____

_____

_____

_____

Spend a few minutes praying and/or journaling about the ways in which God has set you free.

How does your freedom in Christ motivate you toward serving others?

_____

_____

_____

_____

We serve because we're joyful.

Are you joyful? What is the evidence?

_____

_____

_____

Spend a few minutes praying and/or journaling about the reasons for your joy, your struggles in finding joy, and your hopes regarding joy.

How does joy motivate you toward serving others?

_____

_____

_____

We serve because we're loved.

Spend a few minutes praying and/or journaling about God's great love for you. What are your favorite things about Gods love?

_____

_____

_____

How does God's love motivate you toward serving others?

_____

_____

_____

Discovering Revolutionary Contribution

David and His Subjects: Real-Life Revolutionaries

At the end of King David's reign and life, he knew that his work would be unfinished. For years he had planned and dreamed of building a temple for the worship of God. Blessed with abundance in wealth, and rich in experiences with God, David had big ideas about building a place to honor his King. He planned and prepared, commissioning stonecutters, providing iron and lumber and bronze. He drew up plans with precise measurements for a temple unmatched in its splendor and magnificence. And then God told him that he would not be allowed to build the temple. That responsibility would pass to his son, Solomon. So David turned over to Solomon all his plans, entrusting the desires and dreams of his heart, the time and effort he had poured into the project into someone else's hands.

Read the rest of the story in 1 Chronicles 29:1-20.

How would you describe David's contribution to the building of the temple?

_____

_____

_____

_____

What is the question David asked the people in verse 5?

_____

_____

_____

_____

To consecrate means to regard as separate or set apart; or to dedicate something to a sacred purpose. What connection is there between consecrating yourself and making a contribution to the work of God?

_____

_____

_____

_____

The people's contribution to the building of the temple was extraordinary. Using today's measurements, they presented more than 190 tons of gold, 374 tons of silver, 675 tons of bronze, and 3,750 tons of iron to the building project! This is in addition to the 110 tons of gold, 260 tons of silver, and wood and precious stones David had already contributed. Pause for a moment and consider the scope of this building project and the massive amount of resources contributed and put to use!

The Israelites here have much to teach us about the ways we can contribute to "God's projects" in our world. Though we may not be called upon to construct anything like the temple David designed and Solomon constructed, believers are undoubtedly called to contribute to God's work in various ways and through various means. Though their giving was remarkable in its magnitude, the manner in which the Israelites gave is actually more important than the amount they gave, and believers today do well to follow their example.

What do we learn from verses 6 and 9 about the manner in which the Israelites gave?

_____

_____

_____

_____

Why is it important that believers contribute to the work of God willingly?

_____

_____

_____

_____

Does a willing attitude require any sacrifice on the giver's part?

_____

_____

_____

_____

What does David say in verse 14 about the people's giving?

_____

_____

_____

_____

How would you define "generous?"

_____

_____

_____

_____

What kind of sacrifices does generosity require?

_____

_____

_____

_____

Your Real-Life Revolution

To be sure, opportunities for giving surround us. We don't have to look too far to see desperate needs, worthy causes, and projects that deserve attention. How does a believer choose when, where, and how much to give? Again, we are wise to follow the example of the Hebrew people in their giving to the temple.

Write down the question David asked the people, in 1 Chronicles 29:5.

_____

_____

_____

_____

This is without a doubt the place to start! A recognition of your place in God's kingdom and your purpose in his plans will guide your giving well.

Read Ephesians 2:10. What is one purpose God has for you?

_____

_____

_____

_____

Read Romans 12:1-2.

Recalling the earlier definition of "consecrating," how does this passage define consecrating yourself?

_____

_____

_____

_____

What practical things can you do to follow these commands?

_____

_____

_____

_____

How does the idea of consecrating yourself to God's purposes, setting yourself apart to be pleasing to him, affect your view of giving to his work in the world?

_____

_____

_____

_____

The Israelites also gave willingly. What does 2 Corinthians 8:12 teach about this principle?

_____

_____

_____

_____

Read 2 Corinthians 9:7.

Rather than an amount, what parameters define how much a person should give?

_____

_____

_____

_____

What are the two ways God says a person should not give?

_____

_____

_____

_____

What kind of giver is commended?

_____

_____

_____

_____

What adjectives would best describe the manner in which you tend to give? Cheerfully? Willingly? Hesitantly? Dutifully? Use your own words.

_____

_____

_____

_____

Describe a time when you gave with great joy. What were the circumstances and results-in your life and for the recipient(s)?

_____

_____

_____

_____

_____

Would a commitment to willing giving affect your decisions about how, when, and where you would give?

_____

_____

Finally, we can follow the Israelites' example in giving generously. What principle is given in 2 Corinthians 9:6?

_____

_____

_____

_____

2 Corinthians 9:8 establishes the guiding principle that enables believers to be generous. What is it?

_____

_____

_____

_____

How have you seen generous giving in action? Were you the giver, the recipient, or an observer? Describe what you experienced.

_____

_____

_____

_____

Why should Christians give generously?

_____

_____

_____

_____

How do you decide who receives your contributions, and how much you will give? As 2 Corinthians 9:7 says, it ought to be the private conclusion of a surrendered heart. Spend some time in prayer, particularly about the needs you know of in the following areas, and the ways you ought to contribute.

Contributing to the work of God in your church—

What needs do you see?

_____

_____

_____

Is God calling you to give in some way? How?

_____

_____

_____

Contributing to the work of God in your community—

What needs do you see?

_____

_____

_____

Is God calling you to give in some way? How?

_____

_____

_____

Contributing to work of God around the world—

What needs do you see?

_____

_____

_____

Is God calling you to give in some way? How?

_____

_____

_____

Contributing to the work of God in individual lives—

What needs do you see?

_____

_____

_____

Is God calling you to give in some way? How?

_____

_____

_____

Discovering Revolutionary Witness

Philip: Real-Life Revolutionary

According to the book of Acts, in the early days of Christianity the believers in Jerusalem faced severe persecution. Following the martyrdom of Stephen, Acts says that the persecution became so intense that "all except the apostles were scattered throughout Judea and Samaria." This was the height of Saul's tyranny against Christians, and by all accounts it was a frightening and terrible time. But just as God's enemies believed they had won by crucifying Jesus, the persecution and the scattering it caused proved to be exactly what God had ordained!

Read Acts 1:8, Jesus' parting words to the believers gathered with him before his return to heaven. Where did Jesus say they would take the message about him?

_____

_____

_____

_____

Read the result of the scattering recorded in Acts 8:4.

No one could stop these new believers from sharing God's truth wherever they went! The Book of Acts is inspiring in its accounts of empowered, enthusiastic,

Spirit-filled Christians spreading the Good News like wildfire! As believers today we can learn much from the example of those saints of the first century. The same God saves us and the same Spirit fills us. Let's take the unchanging message of his gospel to our world as they did!

One of those saints, Philip, was a revolutionary witness in his day. You've actually studied Philip already in this book, though you may not remember. Read Acts 6:1-6. Where have you seen him before?

_____

_____

_____

_____

When the Jerusalem believers were scattered, where did Philip go? Read Acts 8:5.

_____

_____

_____

_____

According to Acts 8:6-13, what kind of ministry did Philip have in the city of Samaria?

_____

_____

_____

_____

What instruction was Philip given in Acts 8:26?

_____

_____

_____

_____

Compare the place Philip had been ministering to the place he had been called.

_____

_____

_____

_____

Philip had been ministering in the city, with great results! Then God called him to a desert road. Read the rest of the story in Acts 8:27-40.

Write down everything you observe about the person Philip met, in verses 27-28.

_____

_____

_____

_____

What was Philip instructed to do, in verse 29?

_____

_____

_____

_____

How did Philip respond (verse 30)?

_____

_____

_____

_____

The exchange that follows between Philip and the Ethiopian eunuch is fascinating and inspiring. To this point, Philip has experienced a few things the average Western Christian doesn't: severe persecution, displacement, and a visit from an angel of the Lord with instructions to go to a desert road! But from this point in Acts on, everything Philip does is something we can do, too!

What did Philip observe about the Ethiopian, in verse 30?

_____

_____

_____

_____

Read Acts 8:30-35, and summarize in your own words what took place.

_____

_____

_____

_____

_____

What was the first thing Philip said to this man?

_____
_____
_____
_____

How is Philip's approach different from some common, Western approaches to evangelism?

_____
_____
_____
_____

How did the eunuch respond to Philip's question (verse 31-34)?

_____
_____
_____

What does verse 35 say Philip did?

_____
_____
_____

Why did Philip begin with "that very passage?"

_____
_____
_____

What did Philip do next, as recorded in Acts 8:36-38?

_____

_____

_____

_____

Philip was first and foremost obedient to God. He was prepared to proclaim Christ wherever he was sent. When God told him to go, he ran! And when given the opportunity to share the gospel, he did so with gentleness, respect, and clarity. He asked questions instead of shouting answers, he identified the eunuch's current interest and understanding and started there, and he walked with the man in his first steps of obedience. That is revolutionary witness! And we can do it, too!

Your Real-Life Revolution

What do you find most inspiring about Philip's story?

_____

_____

_____

_____

In what ways do you envision following his example?

_____

_____

_____

_____

Do you sense a call to share Christ with others? How do you generally respond to that call?

_____
_____
_____
_____
_____

What encourages you the most in sharing your faith with others?

_____
_____
_____
_____
_____

What hinders or discourages you?

_____
_____
_____
_____
_____

What do these verses say to you about giving away your faith?

Luke 5:31

_____
_____
_____

Romans 10:14

_____
_____
_____

2 Corinthians 5:14

_____
_____
_____

2 Corinthians 5:20

_____
_____
_____

1 Peter 3:15

_____
_____
_____

Philip (and to be sure, many other scattered believers in that day) ministered to the people in front of him, whether he was in Jerusalem, Samaria, or on the desert road. Who are you aware of, in your circle of influence, who does not know Jesus as Savior?

_____
_____
_____
_____
_____

Following Philip's example, how could you do the following with the person(s) you know who do not know Jesus?

Philip heard the man reading Isaiah the prophet and asked him if he understood it.

What do you know about that person's spiritual background and understanding? Did they grow up in the faith? Have they been hurt or turned off by churches or Christians in the past?

_____

_____

_____

_____

If you don't know, ask! People are always experts about themselves—it's hard to stump them or scare them away just by asking questions that show a personal interest.

Philip responded to the eunuch's interest in Isaiah, and explained the gospel from that perspective.

Is there a similar point of entry in your friend's life? If so, what is it?

_____

_____

_____

_____

How could you take his or her current interests and knowledge in spiritual things and begin to present the gospel?

_____

_____

_____

_____

_____

Philip answered the eunuch's questions.

Are you prepared to answer questions? Do you think the non-Christian people you know would feel comfortable asking you questions about your faith?

_____

_____

_____

Besides Philip's initial question, the rest of the conversation is driven primarily by the Ethiopian eunuch. What would it look like for you to follow that pattern with non-Christians you know? Do you think it would be effective?

_____

_____

_____

_____

Write out Colossians 4:5-6 here.

_____

_____

_____

_____

_____

_____

Spend some time in prayer about the people you know who do not know Christ. Pray for wisdom and boldness in being a revolutionary witness for Christ!

Discovering Revolutionary Compassion

Boaz: Real-Life Revolutionary

During the time of the judges in Israel, three women in one family were widowed within a short time. A woman named Naomi lost her husband and her two sons. Her two daughters-in-law grieved as widows alongside her. Thrown into the same boat, the three women were forced to make difficult decisions about their futures. A widow, and particularly one without sons, faced grim and uncertain days in that time and culture. Widows were among the most vulnerable members of society. Decent people took pity on them, but the wicked would take advantage of them. A widow required the compassion of others just to survive. The Book of Ruth tells the beautiful story of Naomi and one of her daughters-in-law, Ruth. Together, the two widows faced their difficult circumstances and cared for one another emotionally, spiritually, and physically. In their story, we see deep compassion for one another—the kind of compassion that is born of shared misery. But we also see another kind of compassion, shown by a man named Boaz.

Naomi and Ruth had left the land of Moab to return to Naomi's hometown of Bethlehem. There they began to establish a new life for themselves. One day soon after their arrival Ruth went to find grain in the fields from the "gleanings" that farmers would leave of their crop for the poor and needy, a custom established in

God's Law (see Leviticus 19:9, Deuteronomy 24:19-22).

Read Ruth 2:3-18.

How did Boaz show compassion to Ruth?

_____

_____

_____

_____

What motivated Boaz to show compassion to Ruth (see verse 11)?

_____

_____

_____

_____

What are three words you would use to describe Ruth?

_____

_____

_____

What are three words you would use to describe Boaz?

_____

_____

_____

Read Ruth 2:9-10. Write down every way you see Boaz acting compassionately toward Ruth. What actions did he take?

_____

_____

_____

_____

What compassionate actions did Boaz take, according to verses 14-15?

_____

_____

_____

_____

Ruth was completely at Boaz's mercy. Had she wandered into a different field, the results could have been quite different. She could have met an unmerciful owner who would have punished her, she might have been unsafe and vulnerable to attack in the fields, and she most certainly would not have been invited to eat until she was full! But Boaz took great steps to protect her and provide for her. He ensured that she was physically safe and supplied; and he preserved her dignity at the same time.

In our society today, and particularly in your own community, who are the "widows and aliens?" Who are the most vulnerable members of society, the most in need of acts of compassion?

_____

_____

_____

_____

_____

_____

Your Real-Life Revolution

Read the following verses and record the attributes and/or actions of God listed alongside his compassion.

Psalm 103:4

_____

_____

_____

_____

Psalm 103:8

_____

_____

_____

_____

Psalm 1116:5

_____

_____

_____

_____

Psalm 145:9

_____

_____

_____

_____

Isaiah 30:18

_____

_____

_____

_____

Matthew 14:14

_____

_____

_____

_____

2 Corinthians 1:3

_____

_____

_____

_____

What instructions are believers given in the following verses?

Zechariah 7:9

_____
_____
_____
_____

Colossians 3:12

_____
_____
_____
_____

1 Peter 3:8

_____
_____
_____
_____

There are a number of qualities that seem conjoined to compassion: grace, mercy, justice, kindness, humility, among others. Choose one of the qualities you discovered in the verses above, and find at least one example or instruction related to that quality in Scripture.

_____
_____
_____
_____

Why did you choose that particular quality? How can you apply compassion and that attribute in a specific and practical way in your life?

_____

_____

_____

_____

_____

The chapter in your reading identifies four focuses of compassion: compassion for the lost, for the poor, for the hurting, and the helpless. Prayerfully consider each one, and write down any opportunities you know you have to show compassion in each respect.

Compassion for the lost

_____

_____

_____

Compassion for the poor

_____

_____

_____

Compassion for the hurting

_____

_____

_____

Compassion for the helpless

_____

_____

_____

I like the way that Webster's *defines compassion: "Sorrow for the sufferings or troubles of another or others, accompanied by an urge to help." The last phrase is especially significant:* accompanied by an urge to help. *The truly compassionate person is motivated to act, to respond with genuine help. Compassion is not merely feeling pity for someone in need, it is doing something to intercede on that person's behalf and meet that need.* (Revolutionary Generosity, pg. 109)

Choose one way this week that you could practice this kind of revolutionary compassion. Write down your intentions here.

_____

_____

_____

Why not make this a regular practice? Write down the opportunities and the needs you see, and make a plan for showing real compassion.

_____

_____

_____

Discovering Revolutionary Generosity

Gaius: Real-Life Revolutionary

You may not be familiar with his name, but an entire book of the Bible was written to and primarily about him. Tucked near the back of your New Testament is a personal note, short on words but long on encouragement, written from John the Apostle to Gaius. In this letter (3 John), the apostle commends Gaius for his faithful hospitality to fellow believers, specifically church leaders who had stayed with him on their travels. Gaius is an example of generosity in action. Whether he gave financially is never specified in 3 John, but as we know, the principles of generosity apply to all types of giving—of money, time, possessions, spiritual gifts, and much more.

Read the epistle of 3 John.

What do we learn about the character of Gaius in verse 3?

_____

_____

_____

_____

_____

_____

_____

Read verses 5-6 and record everything you observe about Gaius' hospitality.

_____

_____

_____

_____

_____

_____

Gaius possessed the fundamental qualities of revolutionary generosity identified in your reading: a noble spirit, a kind heart, and the determination to act.

A Noble Spirit

"It gave me great joy to have some brothers come and tell about your faithfulness to the truth and how you continue to walk in the truth"

2 Peter 1:5-7 provides a good description of the noble believer. Read those verses now, then write your own definition of each quality.

Faith

_____

_____

Goodness

_____

_____

Knowledge

_____

_____

Self-control

_____

_____

Perseverance

_____

_____

Godliness

_____

_____

Brotherly kindness

_____

_____

Love

_____

_____

What does 2 Peter 1:8 say the possession of these qualities produces?

_____

_____

A Kind Heart

"Dear friend, you are faithful in what you are doing for the brothers, even though they are strangers to you. They have told the church about your love."

The apostle Paul certainly expressed kindness to the churches he established and encouraged on his journeys. To be sure, he also exercised authority, he rebuked, and warned, but his love for believers is indisputable. Read Paul's own words about kindness in action in 1 Thessalonians 2:7-12.

Write down all the character qualities of kindness you see recorded.

_____

_____

_____

_____

_____

_____

Read Ephesians 2:7 and Titus 3:4. How does Jesus express God's kindness to you?

_____

_____

_____

_____

_____

_____

According to Galatians 5:22, what is the source of kindness in a believer's life?

_____

_____

_____

_____

A Determination to Act

"You are faithful in what you are doing for the brothers...you will do well to send them on their way in a manner worthy of God...we ought therefore to show hospitality to such men so that we may work together for the truth."

Read and meditate on 1 John 3:18.

The Book of James speaks to the intrinsic connection between faith and action. Read James 2:14-17. What do you believe it means that faith that is not accompanied by action is dead?

_____

_____

_____

_____

What does Ephesians 2:10 have to say on this topic?

_____

_____

_____

_____

Your Real-Life Revolution

What do you believe revolutionary generosity would look like in your life? What are the specific opportunities you would seize and needs you would meet if you really gave in revolutionarily generous ways?

_____

_____

_____

_____

_____

What hinders your generosity?

_____

_____

_____

_____

What encourages you toward generosity?

_____

_____

_____

_____

Who do you know with a noble and generous spirit?

_____

_____

_____

_____

Who do you know with a kind and generous heart?

_____

_____

_____

_____

Who do you know with a generosity that leads to deci-
sive action?

_____

_____

_____

_____

What could you do to imitate and to glean from each
of the people you listed above?

_____

_____

_____

_____

"Taking hold of the life that is truly life."

Read 1 Timothy 6:17-19.

Would you consider yourself "rich in this present
world?" If so, why? If not, why not?

_____

_____

_____

_____

_____

What is the three-fold command you have been given in verse 18?

_____

_____

_____

_____

_____

_____

Reflect on those commands for a few minutes, and then write down one or two ways you can obey them in the coming days.

Do good—

_____

_____

_____

_____

Be rich in good deeds—

_____

_____

_____

_____

Be generous and willing to share—

_____

_____

_____

_____

What do you believe it means to "take hold of the life that is truly life?"

_____

_____

_____

_____

_____

"True generosity is both a quality and a practice. It is a quality void of complaint, full of gratitude and driven by concern. And it is a practice that will not let one sit still and do nothing while others are in need."
(Revolutionary Generosity, pg. 126)

Spend some time in prayer, considering the quality of generosity.

Are you reflecting God's generosity in the ways you give to others? How?

_____

_____

_____

_____

Generally speaking, are you more prone to complain or to be grateful?

_____

_____

_____

_____

What concerns do you have about needs you see?

_____

_____

_____

_____

How could you be more generous?

_____

_____

_____

_____

What is the next step you're going to take toward becoming a generous revolutionary?

_____

_____

_____

_____

_____

_____